Blouse Pattern Pizazz

with Shirley Adams

A common sense approach is used throughout this book to take the mystery and presumed difficulty out of changing simple patterns to whatever designs you want. Armed with the knowledge contained herein, you can have the most wildly original blouse wardrobe your creative imagination will permit. Every blouse design possibility is not detailed for that would build an enormous volume. Any type change is suggested however, from which you can see how other variations might be accomplished. Move on to making changes in other types of basic patterns such as pants and skirts.

After many years as a university clothing professor, I now take great delight in teaching home sewers to sew creatively. Throw out some of the tedious rules formerly learned as you realize other ways may work just as well and perhaps better. Free yourself from the dependency on pattern guide sheets as you think through logically what must be done first, what second, etc. Cut up copies of the page 2 miniature blouse pattern as you figure out other adaptations on your own, then use these mini changes as your personal guidesheets. Begin a looseleaf notebook of magazine clippings with the mini pattern adaptations and keep it all bound together as your treasure chest of future projects.

This book was written originally, and now revised, expanded, reformatted in response to countless requests expressed. Many thanks to those viewers of my first PBS series "THE NEEDLE AND EYE", the second series "...AND SEW ON", the whole family of ongoing "THE SEWING CONNECTION" series, and participants in live seminars.

Have fun with your craft!

Shirley Adams

Shirley Adams Publications
922 Cheltenham Way
Plainfield, IN 46168

TABLE OF CONTENTS

PATTERN CHOICE AND CORRECTION 1

MINIATURE BLOUSE PATTERN 2

MAKING A PERMANENT PATTERN 6

DESIGNING OTHERS FROM BASIC 6

FABRIC CONSIDERATIONS 7

METHODS OF CHANGING BASIC 8

BLOUSE CLOSURES 9
Front Band 9
Attached Facing Band 10
Separate Facing 10
Back Neck Facing 11
Bias Facing 11
Bias Binding 11
Concealed Placket 11
Exposed facing 12
Double Breasted 12
Assymetrical Closing 12
Surplice 13
Shoulder closing 13
Back Neck Closing 14

BODICE INTERIOR CHANGES 15
Vertical Tucking 15
Horizontal Tucks 17
Pleat First, Then Cut 18
Bibs 19
Diagonal Tucks 20
Harlequin Pintucking 20
Pulled Threads 20
Sunburst Tucks or Gathers 21
Shoulder Gathers 22
Shoulder Yoke 23
Separate Yokes 23
Assymetrical Drapes 24
Pockets 24
Patch Pockets 25
Buttonhole Pockets 25
In-seam Pockets 26
Flying Layers 27
Shoulder Epaulets 27
Shoulder Pad Space 27
Lace or Eyelet Insertions 28
Ruffles and Flounces 28
Combining Pattern Pieces 29
Overblouse Waistband 29
Dresses 29

NECKLINES 30
Changing Shape 30
Bateau 32
Cowl 33
Deep Cowl 33
Two-piece Cowl 34

COLLARS 34
Full-roll 34
Convertible 35
Two-piece 35
Mandarin 36
Wingtip 36
Shawl 36
Tie Collar 37
Ascot Effect 37

Fitted, Flat, Shaped 38
Sailor 38
Ruffled 38
Ruffled on V Neck 39
Collars on Lowered Neck 39
Double Layer Collar 39

Bias Collars 40
Turtle Neck 40
Cowl Collar 40
Funnel Collar 40
Sashed Buttonhole 41

SLEEVES 41
Set-in 41
Elasticized Wrist 42
Horizontal Tucks 42
Roll-up 43
Short Sleeves 43
Button Wrist, No Cuff 43
Full Gathers at Wrist 44
Pleats at Wrist 44
Narrow Wrist 44
Seamed Leg-o-mutton 44
Puffed Variation 45
Petal or Tulip 45
Puffed at Cap 46
Full Cap and Wrist 46
Lace Insets 46
Vertical Pleats 46
Pleated Cap 47
Deeply Pleated Cap 47
Square Armhole 47

Set-in Sleeves cont.
   Pointed Under Armscye   48
   Dropped Shoulders   48
   Cap Sleeved Blouses   49
   Opening Above Wristband   52
   Varying Cuff Depth   52
   French Cuffs   52

   Raglan Sleeves   53
   Yoked Raglan   54
   Square-cornered Raglan   54
   Peasant Blouse   55

   Kimono Sleeves   55
   Gussets   56
   Straight Cut Shoulder   56
   Banded Kimono   57
   One-piece Blouse   58

PATTERNLESS BLOUSES   59

ADD-ON ACCESSORIES   65

SPECIAL TECHNIQUES   73

A blouse was formerly considered a fashion accessory to go with a suit. But that blouse has come into its own, taken on new emphasis and importance and can now set the tone for the rest of what you wear. The fact that it's closest to your face makes it the most visible part of your costume.

Its versatility lends easily to day or evening wear depending on its fabric and style, on the skirt or pants, and the jewelry worn with it. Its lack of bulk means several blouses might replace the space of one dress in a suitcase greatly expanding a travel wardrobe. Its relatively smaller cost makes it compatible with any budget.

BLOUSE PATTERN CHOICE AND CORRECTION

The place to begin is in choosing a good basic pattern, perhaps one you already own which fits just the way you like it. This should be a tailored style with a front buttoned closing, a collar, long set-in sleeves something like the following sketch. The fit is personal preference for women's blouse fashions haven't the more rigid standards of men's tailored shirts.

To help solidify your thoughts on fit, let me list my personal preferences as a starting point and then you can agree and conform, or disagree and make changes accordingly. I like a blouse to fit as the word implies...blousey rather than snug. The sketch illustrates a type appropriate for a basic and the labels indicate my personal check points. The fashion pendulum swings from tighter to looser and back through the years so preferences then change accordingly.

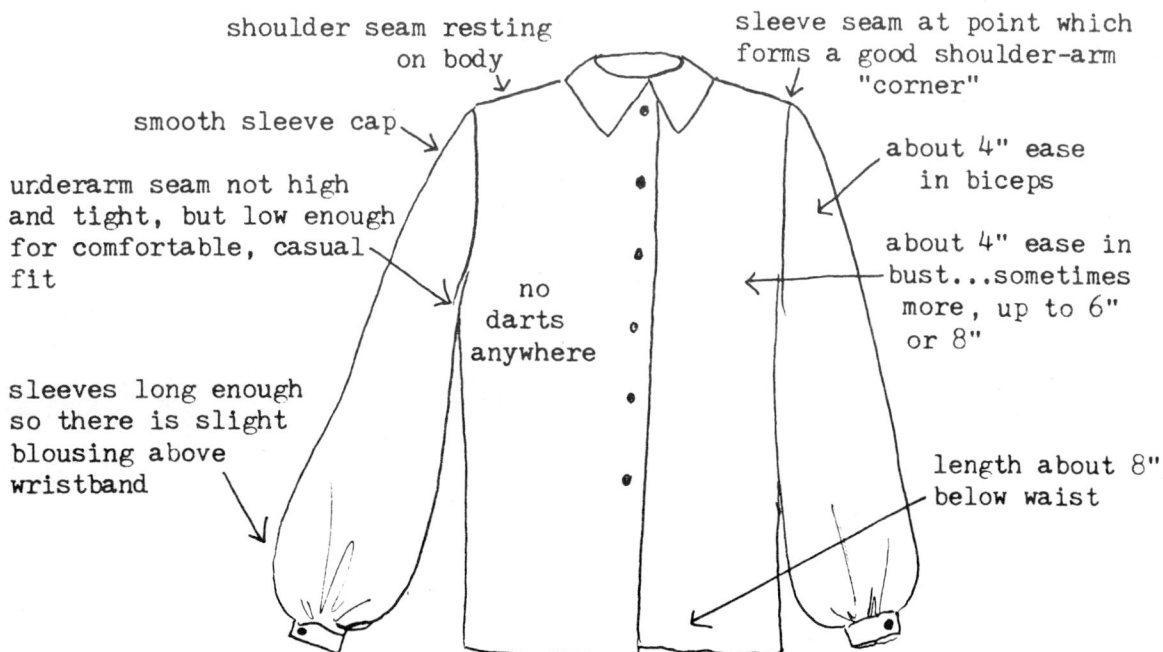

shoulder seam resting on body

sleeve seam at point which forms a good shoulder-arm "corner"

smooth sleeve cap

underarm seam not high and tight, but low enough for comfortable, casual fit

about 4" ease in biceps

about 4" ease in bust...sometimes more, up to 6" or 8"

no darts anywhere

sleeves long enough so there is slight blousing above wristband

length about 8" below waist

1/4 size pattern on which to try out changes.

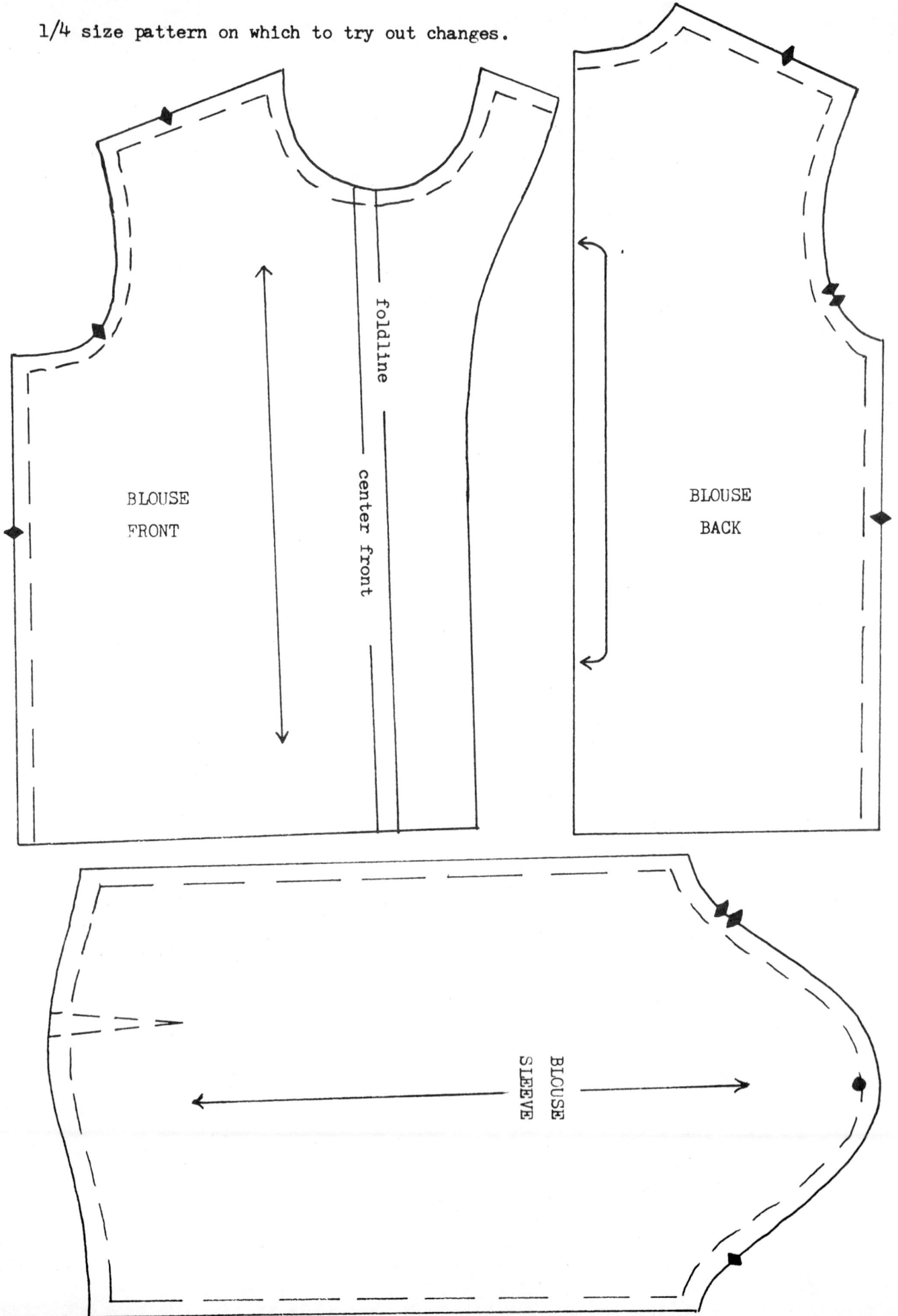

BLOUSE FRONT

foldline

center front

BLOUSE BACK

BLOUSE SLEEVE

Your blouse pattern might have the shoulder seam right on the shoulder, or it might be dropped forward to a yoke line. Either works fine, for to convert one to the other is an easy task as shown.

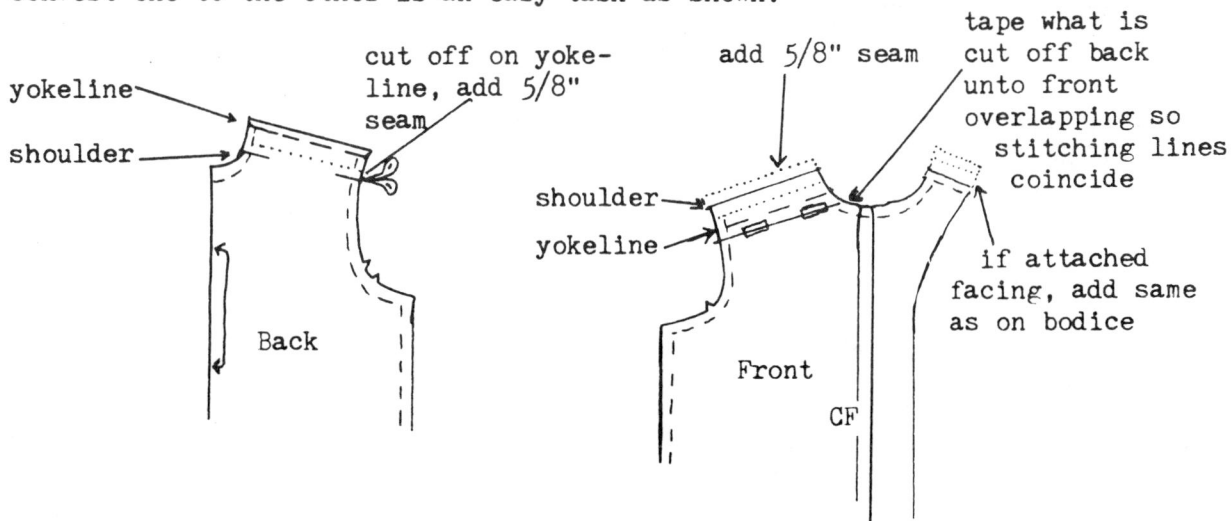

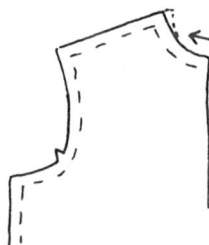

yokeline

shoulder

cut off on yoke-line, add 5/8" seam

Back

add 5/8" seam

tape what is cut off back unto front overlapping so stitching lines coincide

shoulder

yokeline

if attached facing, add same as on bodice

Front

CF

It is likely that a little width may have to be added in front neck as dotted line indicates so that it matches up in shoulder seam length with back when stitching together.

Try on a blouse made from this basic pattern or...if using a new pattern you have never made up...pin together at shoulders and side seams and try on the bodice part of paper pattern. Look at the side view in a mirror. A small, flat bust will permit balanced hanging. A prominent bust will more than likely demand more length and the blouse will hang shorter in front.

This is alright if you always wear it tucked in or belted, blousing it more in back. If however, you ever wear it out and unbelted, you may want to correct the front. This may be accomplished in two ways after determining how much longer the front should be. Do not merely add more front length at the lower hem.

1. Add a dart. While blouse is on the body mark the bust point with a pin. Then correct the pattern front by drawing a horizontal line right at the bust, perpendicular to the grain arrow.

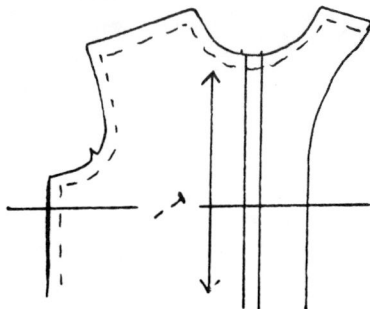

Cut through that line and tape to a paper
insert the width necessary to lengthen
the blouse the proper amount.

Draw a dart whose base is the same
as the paper insert, and whose
point is about one inch short
of your bust point.

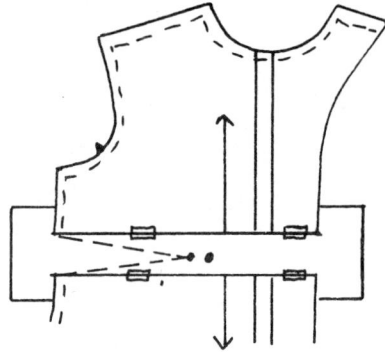

    2. Lengthen front and sleeve
at armscye level. Instead of
correcting at bust level as you
would with a dart, if you want no
darts to appear in the blouse
make correction above...at armscye about where the notch occurs.

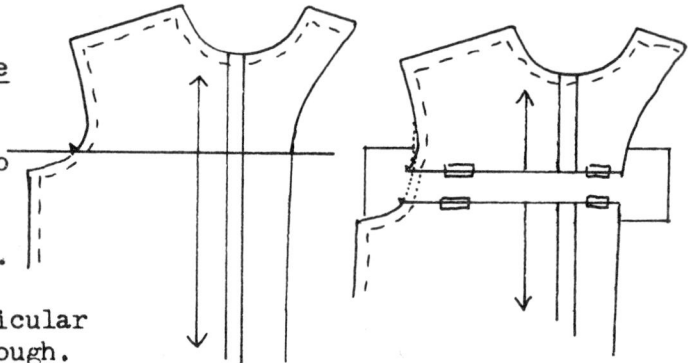

Draw the horizontal line perpendicular
to the grain arrow and slash through.
Insert and tape paper, lengthening
blouse the proper amount and keeping
grain arrow lined up straight.

"True up" armscye seam by penciling
in a smooth line.

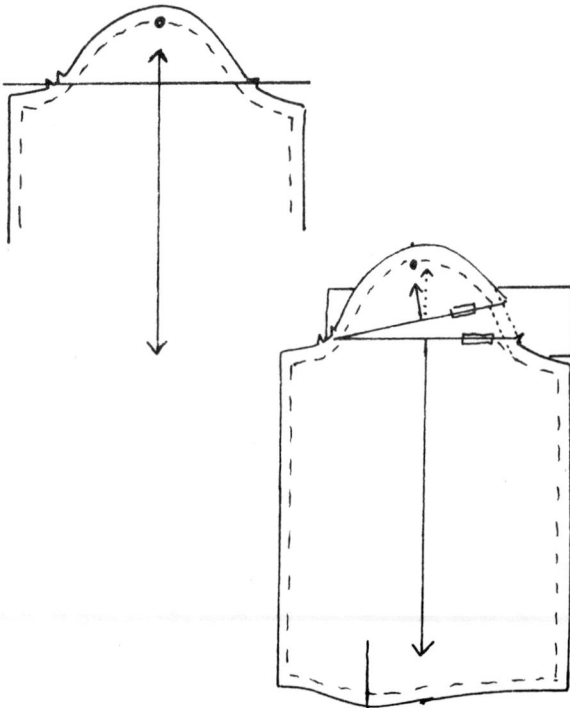

The sleeve will then also need to
be corrected so it will fit when
stitched to bodice. Draw a horizontal line at the sleeve notch.
(Single notch always is seen at
sleeve and bodice fronts, double
notches at back).

Slash to...but not through...sleeve
cap back and insert, tape paper the
same extra length as you added to the
bodice. Correct grain arrow with a
ruler as dotted line indicates.

If the shoulder seam doesn't touch your body smoothly, adjustment may be necessary here.

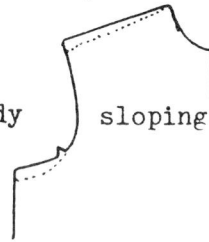

Sloping shoulders need to have seams also slope out toward arms like this sketch. To keep the armscye the same size as the original so the sleeve will still fit in, whatever is cut off the shoulder needs to be cut off under the arm tapering to nothing by the time you reach the notch.

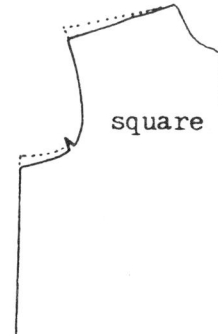

sloping

square

For square shoulders, the reverse is true. Add to both shoulder and underarm whatever is necessary for a smooth, unpulled fit.

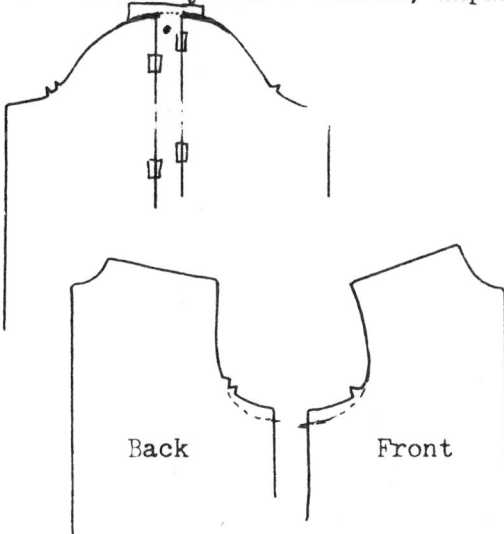

Back   Front

If your upper arm is quite large and your sleeve and armscye bind uncomfortably, enlarge both.

Split the sleeve and add whatever additional inches suitable. Then cut out at underarm of blouse to make it lower and looser, tapering out at notch, so that the larger sleeve will sew in smoothly. Generally this will work if, for example, 2" are added to sleeve, 1" lowering will be necessary in bodice front and back. Measure new stitching lines to be sure it does work.

If your pattern needs more width in bust and hips both, slash from bottom up to shoulder (but not through). Swing out as sketch indicates and tape an insert paper strip to it.

If it needs to be wider at the hips only, this addition may be made on side seams as dotted line indicates.

These same corrections would also be needed on bodice back.

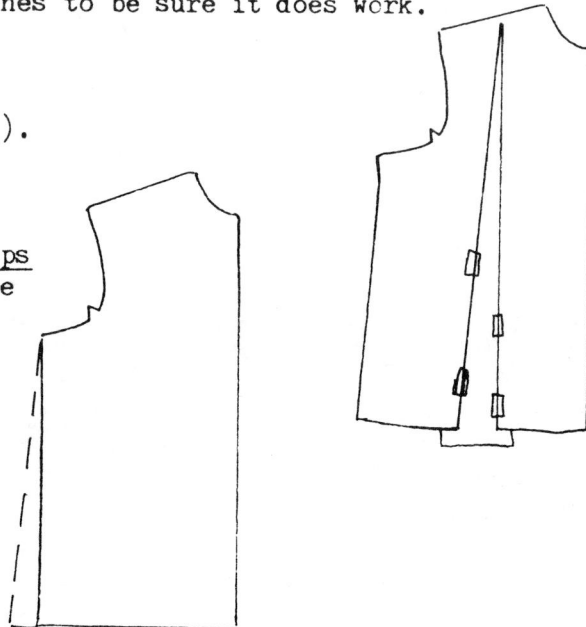

The sleeve may also need correcting.
My personal preference, but not necessarily
yours, is that vertical seams are parallel.
To do this, slash up the center but not
completely through, and swing sides apart
until this is accomplished before
taping in the insert.

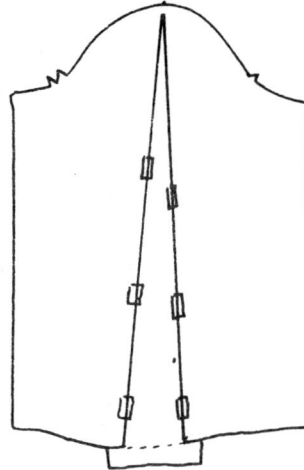

MAKING A PERMANENT PATTERN

Now your blouse pattern is corrected so that the fit is as you prefer.
It may have needed very little change and the paper is in good shape. Or
perhaps you slashed and taped to the extent that it looks like a hopeless
mess! Either way, how many times can you use a tissue pattern before it
completely disintegrates? It may be wise to put it in a more permanent
form which can be used dozens or hundreds of times, staying intact.

My personal preference is to now trace each piece on something lasting
such as a light weight non-woven interfacing fabric like Pellon. Stores
also carry products like Trace-a-Pattern or other brands which are fabric-
like and take hard usage. Put this over your pattern pieces and trace with
a felt tipped pen transferring all labels and markings. Cut out and you
have an indestructible pattern. We have so far only been working with the
three basic blouse main pieces. Later you may wish to put other frequently
used parts (basic collars, cuffs, etc.) in this permanent form.

DESIGNING OTHER BLOUSES FROM YOUR BASIC PATTERN

The starting point is a picture. It may be torn from a magazine or
newspaper, or you may have to sketch one, but you should have a picture
more definite than the one in your mind to refer to when changing the
pattern. There are so many good ideas to be adapted from outside sources,
that it is wise to keep a little sketch pad in your purse to use when out
shopping...or paper and pencil handy where you sit to watch television.
You needn't be an artist. Everyone has the ability to record on paper
the few simple lines which convey the ideas to then make pattern changes
accordingly.

The rest of the book contains ideas for making design changes and
shows how to do them. This most assuredly isn't all-inclusive for you
can let your imagination soar and expand your ability to numerous unlisted
ideas. Fashion through the years will also bring on other changes. This
just serves as a key to unlock those ideas and realize you can do anything
you want...if you just try. Visualize the end result with a sketch, make
the pattern changes, and construct a beautiful one-of-a-kind blouse which
is your own original!

Consider the fabric. Matching up fabrics with intended design is the point at which many would-be designers go wrong. Think over the following suggestions for happier results and beautiful success.

If the blouse will later be dry cleaned you may leave the worries to the professional cleaner. These might include silk or heavy crepe fabrics which you would prefer not to wash. Repeated dry cleaning of white silk however, will probably yellow the fabric eventually. It may be hand washed, rolled in a towel to remove excess moisture, ironed while still quite damp... if you are a gambler which I am. If serious doubts make you hesitate, dry clean as results are not guaranteed. Even I would have this cleaned if complicated details produce an unwillingness to do laborious ironing.

Heavy crepes of silk, acetate, or rayon will shrink with washing... sometimes progressively...so preshrinking will not necessarily do the job. Some of these must be dry cleaned. To test you might cut off a 6" square, wash and dry, re-measure to make a decision.

If a cotton, linen, polyester or other fabric will definitely be machine washed and dried later after it is made up, then wash and dry before cutting out to preshrink, remove excess finishes, and to see how the fabric will turn out. If it comes from the dryer needing a good deal of actual ironing (not just a slight touch-up pressing) make it into a relatively simple style which is easier to take care of. If it exits the dryer looking like it's ready-to-wear, then it would be suitable for more complicated details ...pleats and tucks, ruffles, etc. for its later care will not be a cause for concern.

Fabric hand must also be considered for pleasing results. A crisp fabric is better used in tailored styling. A supple thin fabric will drape nicely in soft feminine styling. Pleats should be stitched down in crisp fabrics but may be unstitched, pressed or unpressed in the soft fabrics.

Interfacing, especially the sheer fusibles, work well in cotton-type fabrics. Silky-type fabrics often are overpowered by fusible interfacing and might be better handled with a third layer of the fashion fabric in collars, cuffs and in buttonhole and button areas.

If any trims are used be sure their care is compatible with the fashion fabric. Also take care that they are preshrunk, fade-proof.

Let's get going on the how-to of making changes with which the rest of the book deals. Because of the very small sketch sizes, there may be slight discrepencies in accuracy of seam lengths, notch locations, etc. The mere width of a pen line can do this. Don't let this disturb you as these illustrations are only meant as instructional how-to. You would not actually be making patterns from them so these imperfections are insignificant. On page 2 is a pattern for the typical basic blouse done in 1/4 size. Duplicate this on a copier and use these mini patterns to try out any desired changes to see how they work out before cutting up a large size pattern.

THREE METHODS OF CHANGING: MOVE-IT-OVER, PIVOT, SLASH

The first two methods can be done directly with your basic pattern. The third method, slash, involves first cutting the basic out in another piece of paper so that it can then be slashed. Avoid cutting into your precious original basic! Each of these methods will be briefly illustrated so that you can understand what is involved.

1. Move-it-over. This can be used when changes are relatively simple and the quickest way to cut the new blouse fabric is to start with your Pellon.

In this sleeve for example, we want to add fullness at both the cap and the wrist to form a pleat. Pin or weight down the pattern to the fabric and cut one half the sleeve as the dark line indicates. Notch top and bottom at sleeve center by making tiny scissor clips.

Then move the pattern over about 4" on the fabric, notch top and bottom again, and finish cutting the other darkened side. This would provide the extra fabric in the center to be later pleated up to the sleeve center.

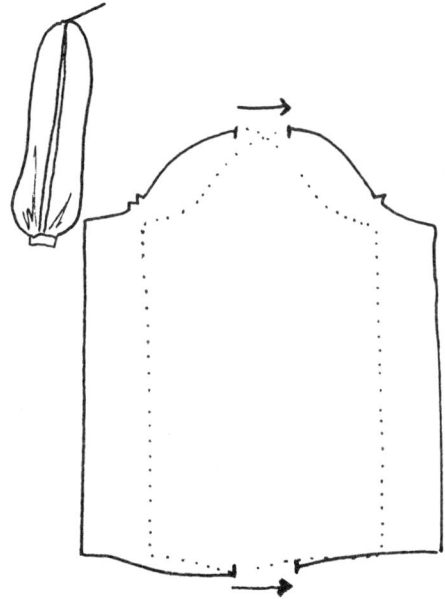

2. Pivot. Let's say that we want a lot of gathering on that sleeve wrist, but want the cap to remain smooth.

Cut out the darkened line, then pivot keeping the cap dot in place, and cut out the other side blending in the bottom line. Mark (with a pin) on the fabric the center of the wrist to know how far from that center line you pivot...equally in both directions.

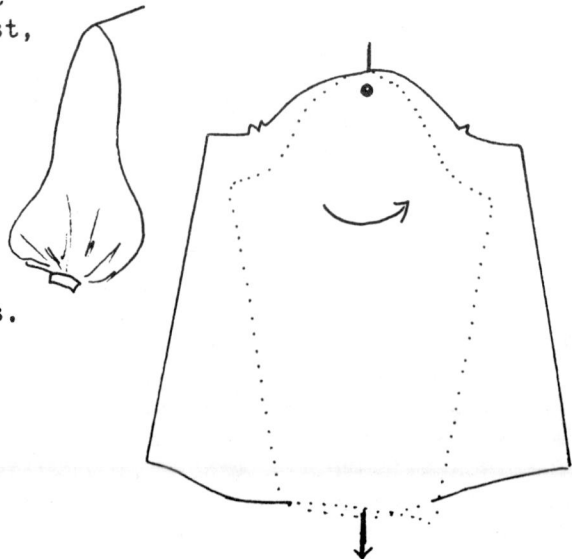

9

3. <u>Slash</u>. Something more complicated will happen necessitating cutting up the pattern. First cut the basic in another piece of paper. The new paper can then be cut up and seams added to make the finished pattern without harming your original.

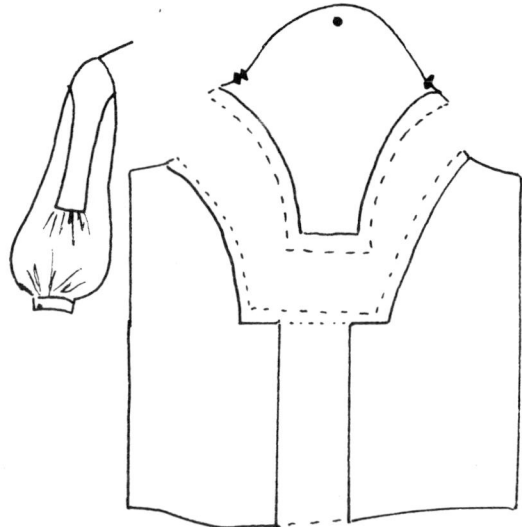

The following page is a miniature (about one forth life size) pattern for a basic blouse. It is included here for your convenience so that as you design you can trace these mini pieces, cut them up, and experiment to figure how you will do the changes before proceding in full size.

BLOUSE CLOSURES

Unless the neckline is low cut enough to slip the blouse over your head, somewhere there must be an opening for getting into and out of the blouse. The most standard is as this basic mini front has, a button down the front closure.

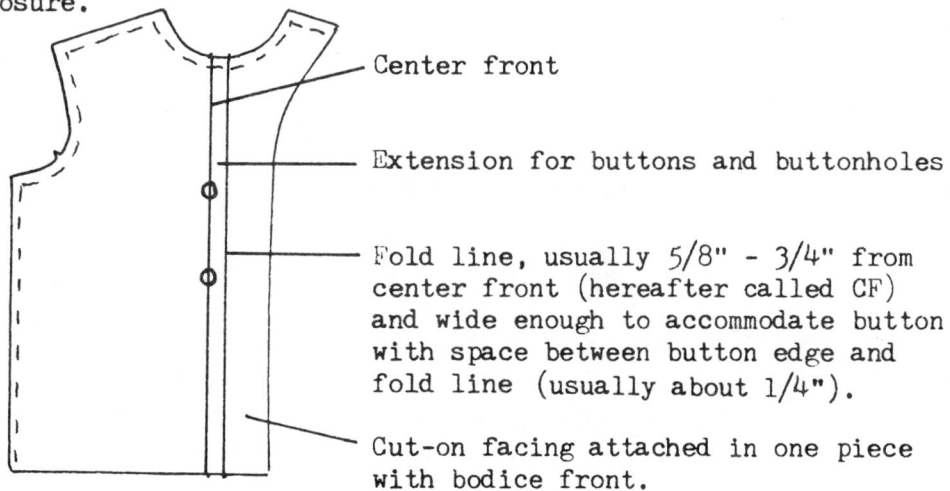

— Center front

— Extension for buttons and buttonholes

— Fold line, usually 5/8" - 3/4" from center front (hereafter called CF) and wide enough to accommodate button with space between button edge and fold line (usually about 1/4").

— Cut-on facing attached in one piece with bodice front.

<u>Front band</u>. An extra front band is sometimes made, possibly as illustrated, to utilize the design feature of contrasting stripes. To make this pattern, draw a rectangular strip the same length as bodice CF. The width would be <u>twice</u> the width from CF to facing foldline <u>plus</u> two seam allowances. This may be cut on fabric's straight, crosswise, or bias.

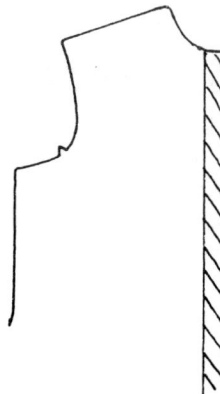

The band's side seams are pressed
under and it is topstitched in place
on <u>right</u> blouse front before facing
is turned back or any other
construction takes place. Facing
is then pressed under before buttonholes
are made through all thicknesses.

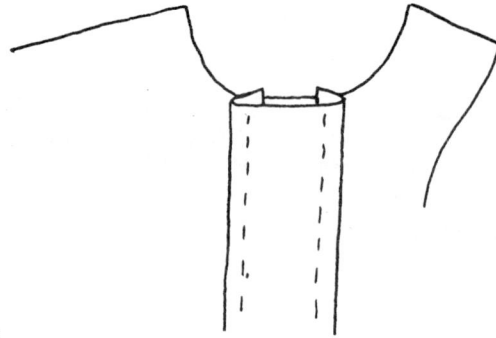

The <u>left</u> blouse front can do without
this added band.

<u>Abbreviated front facing band</u>.
If there is no reason for the
facing to duplicate blouse
neckline all the way up to the
shoulder as on the basic, a
straight cut-on band can be
utilized and cut one width
wider to fold under and act
as a self-interfacing layer.

CF

Fold

Facing band which is
twice width from CF
to fold

Interfacing layer which
duplicates facing if
wanting to avoid inter-
facing of a different
fabric

When all folded in place
and finished, it would
be in this position.

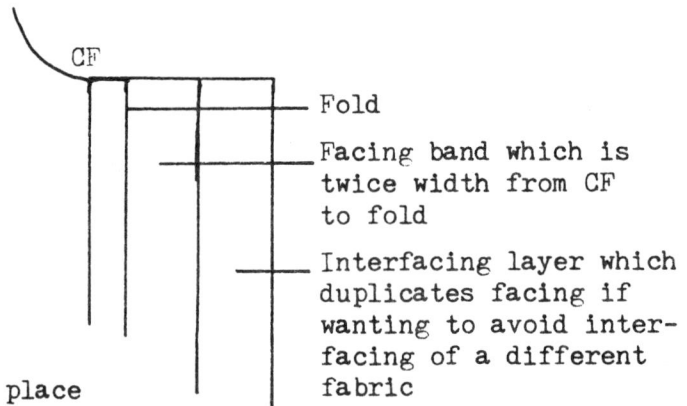

This is especially good on thin, silky, woven fabrics where an
interfacing fabric might overpower the delicate fabric hand. On cottons,
eliminate the interfacing layer of self fabric, and fuse on a separate
interfacing to inside of facing layer for a crisper result.

<u>Separate facing</u>. This must be used when
edge is flared and therefore cannot be a
fold back, cut-on facing. This flaring
would be used on lapels with more width
than the straight, cut-on facing could
provide.

To make, fold back facing on fold
line to get it out of the way since it
will not be used. Cut out fronts with
extra flaring width near neck which tapers
to nothing at breakpoint. Include an
outside seam allowance.

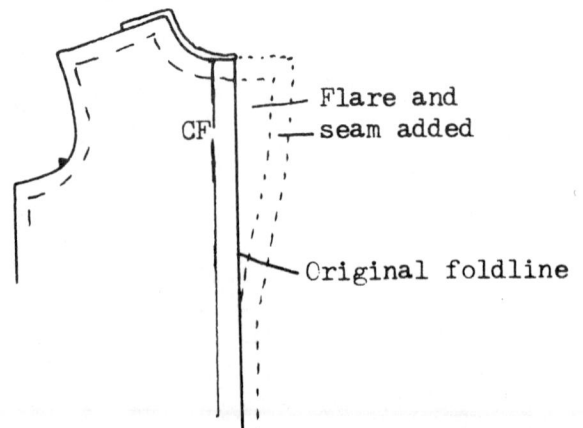

CF

Flare and
seam added

Original foldline

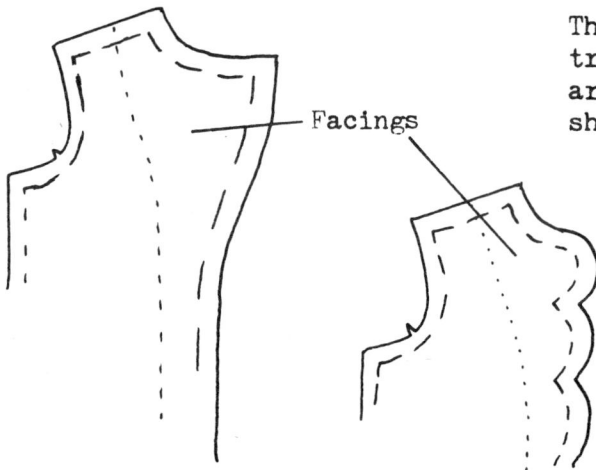

Then cut the new, separate facing by tracing a duplicate of the new front, around the neck and about 3" down the shoulder as the dotted line indicates.

A separate facing would also be necessitated by scallops, or other "different" edge.

Facings

Be sure the shoulder width is equal to that of the front facing.

Back neck facing. The back neck facing is always a separate piece. Just like these fronts, it is made by tracing the neck and partially down the shoulder to be a duplicate of the bodice neckline.

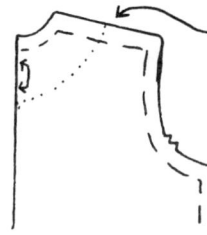

Bias facing. The neck can also be faced by cutting a strip of bias as long as needed CB to CF, and as wide as desired plus seam allowances, rather than the fitted facings.

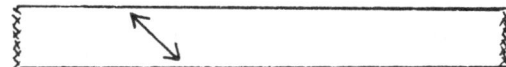

Bias binding. If this is to be a binding showing outside as well as inside the neck edge, cut wider so it can enclose the neck edge. If the fabric is quite thin, cutting this a double width for a double layer of fabric would look richer. Press it in half lengthwise, then stitch the two raw bias edges to the outside of the neckline. Trim off excess neck edge seam allowance, turn double layer to inside of neck and either whip fold of bias down by hand, or ditch stitch it in place by machine.

Concealed placket. If no buttons are to show on the outside, the original cut-on facing can be cut in the fabric and pressed under in place. An additional strip is cut the length of the blouse, twice the placket width, plus seam allowances. It is pressed in half and stitched to blouse front where indicated by dotted line.

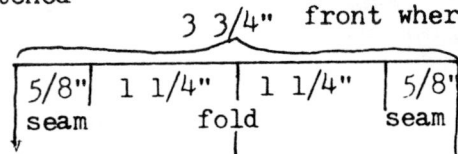

Top layers of blouse pulled back to reveal concealed placket where buttonholes are stitched

3 3/4"

| 5/8" seam | 1 1/4" | 1 1/4" fold | 5/8" seam |

Decorative exposed facing. A facing
needn't hide inside the blouse.
Sometimes a contrasting color or
patterned fabric is used and shows
on the outside. In this case the
right side of the facing is stitched
to the wrong side of the blouse,
around neck and down front seam,
trimmed and turned to outside to
be topstitched or decoratively
trapunto stitched in place.

    By now you surely understand the possibilities of front closures
and their facings. Closures can also be located elsewhere. For all the
following the blouse front has been duplicated on paper to the CF only,
facing eliminated. Separate facings would then be cut later as needed.

VARIATIONS ON CLOSURES

Double breasted. Using the original blouse
front only to its CF, decide how wide an
additional overlap will be. Tape a piece
of paper on for this additional width. The
dotted line sketched indicates the left
blouse front will be a duplicate of the right.

    The wider apart the double breasted
buttons are placed, the wider your body
will also look.

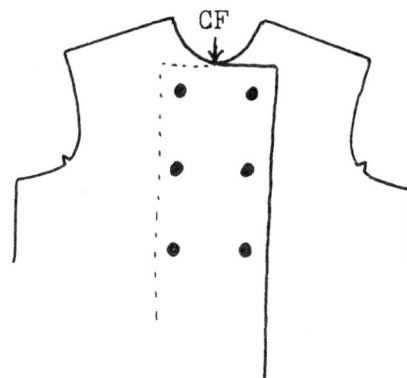

Assymetrical closing. A variation of this
would be to eliminate one row of buttons
(the decorative row on right half of blouse
as it is on your body) and give the
appearance of an assymetrical or off-center
closing, buttoned or tied.

    This pattern can be the same as for
double breasted, or it can be changed
on the right blouse front only, left
front cut just to the CF as dotted
line shows.

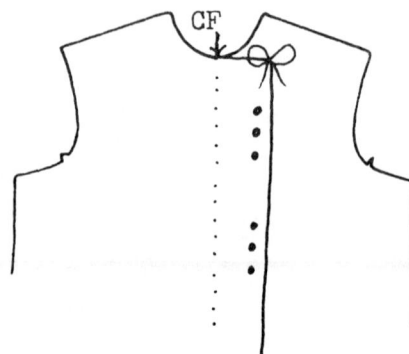

Surplice. This neckline is seen in a wrap blouse or dress and is possibly not fastened except for an inner ribbon tie, snaps, or an outside belt. The pattern is changed by first deciding how low on the center front the point of the V will be. Continue this line down to the side seam maybe making a straight diagonal, maybe a curved diagonal for a more graceful line.

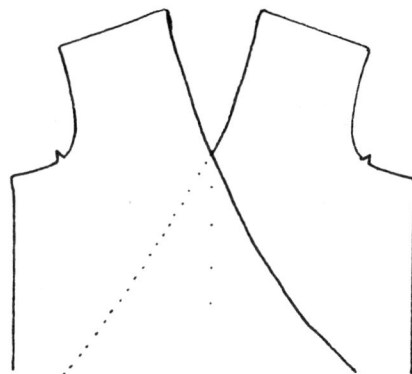

Duplicate for a facing layer, or bind edge with a bias strip.

Because this whole edge is bias, it can stretch out of shape very easily and care must be taken to avoid this.

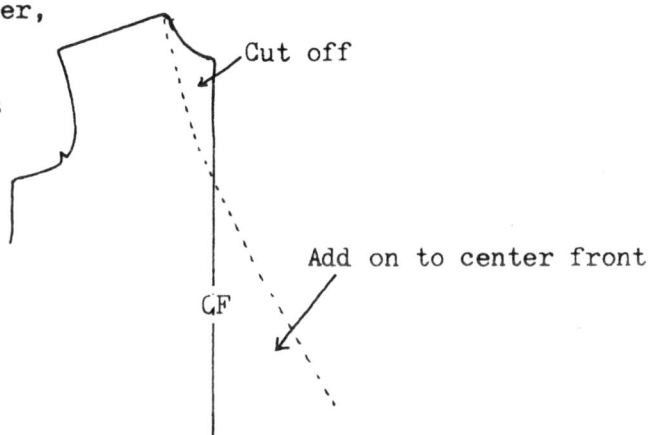

Cut off

Add on to center front

CF

Shoulder closing. This would usually be located on the left shoulder. Tape together two paper fronts at the CF as you will be cutting a single fabric layer (rather than the usual double layers) since the left shoulder is different than the right. The right shoulder remains unchanged as it will be a regular seam. The left shoulder will have an extension added to be turned under at the stitching line for a facing, and again for a self-interfacing.

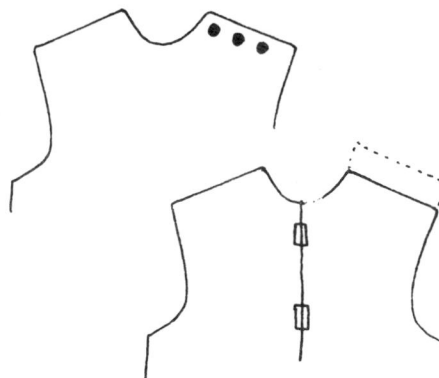

Buttonholes will then be made through these three thick-nesses. An enlargement of that shoulder extension would be:

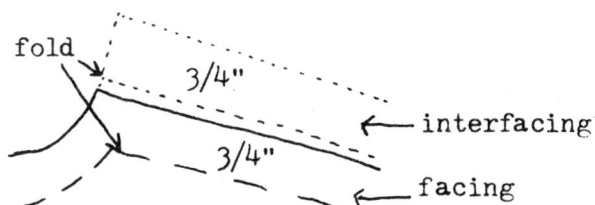

fold

3/4"

3/4"

interfacing

facing

OR, to avoid the necessity of the extra pattern work, use the original pattern cutting the extra shoulder length in double layers. Later trim off the unwanted excess in right shoulder.

Shoulder loops. An alternate way to treat this opening is to cut the left and right shoulders the same (this would mean use only one pattern front and cut fabric double with a CF fold). For the left shoulder cut a facing duplicating the shoulder shape.

Insert buttonhole loops (refer to back of book to learn how to make them) between layers before stitching and turning so then loops stand out from finished edge.

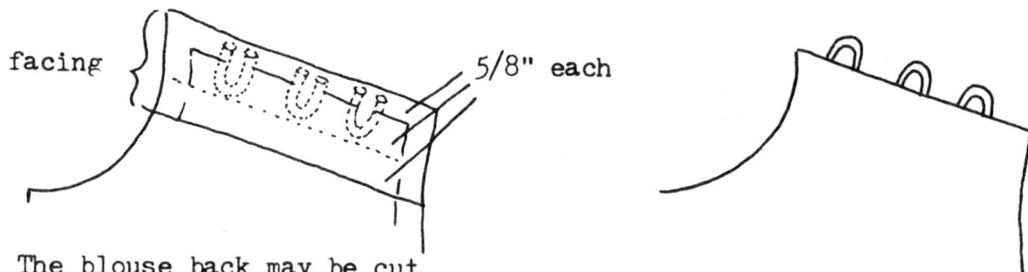

facing   5/8" each

The blouse back may be cut with left shoulder only having a long enough extension to fold under for extra fabric layer, and still underlap the front shoulder enough to sew buttons on it.

This would necessitate using two back bodice pieces taped together at CB so the shoulders could be cut differently and then cutting a single layer of fabric.

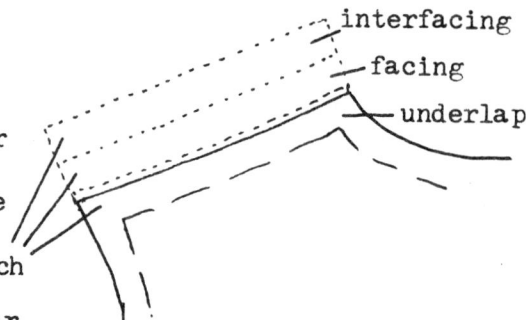

interfacing
facing
underlap

3/4" each

OR, more efficiently, use regular pattern cutting double fabric layers on fold, adding to both shoulders. Later trim off unwanted right shoulder excess.

Back neck closing. This may be as simple as cutting the blouse back on the fold and duplicating the neckline for the facing, but extending the lower edge of facing pattern 2" longer than the desired opening will be. (The curved grain arrow always indicates "cut on fold").

Stitch seam as indicated in illustration, first securing loop buttonholes in place. Slash and trim seam allowances short, clip where necessary. Turn, press, sew on button(s).

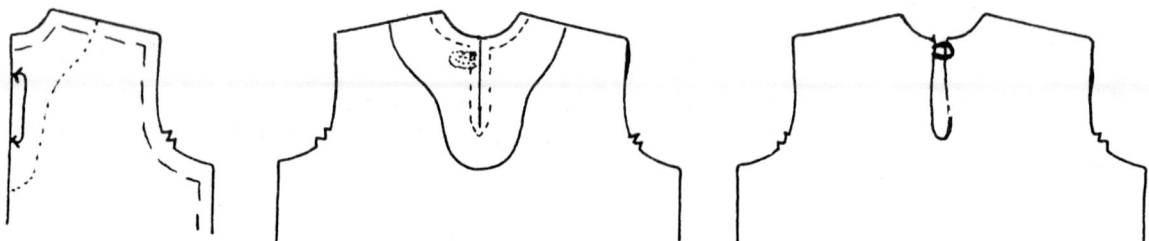

Or the back may instead be cut with a CB seam and an extension added to the top several inches which would be for buttons on the underlapped right extension, buttonholes on the left side.

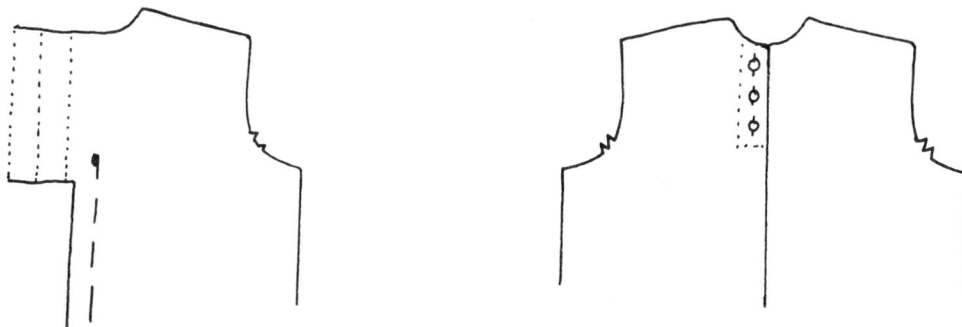

BODICE INTERIOR CHANGES

<u>Vertical</u> <u>tucking</u>. Tucks can occur wherever you desire, can be very narrow or wider, stitched their entire length or only partially. They are usually centered in some way but might just as easily be grouped assymetrically on one side. Just find a picture or draw your sketch first, figure out the means to accomplish the intended end result, and make your pattern possibly by the "move-it-over" technique, more likely by slashing and spreading to produce the extra fabric needed for pleats.

This would be cut on a center front fold, have a back neck opening, and the tucks are fairly wide on my example (maybe an inch) overlapping slightly so that stitching only shows at those closest to the CF when they are pressed in place away from CF.

These could also be pressed flat rather than one-way, using other techniques the same to achieve a different look.

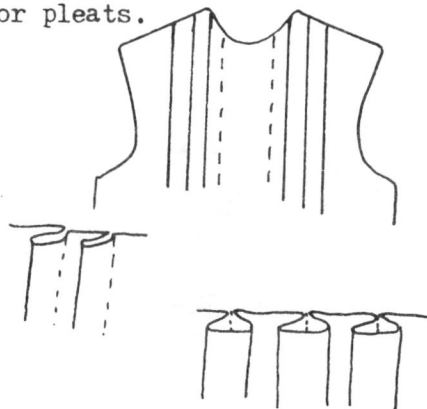

On the pattern, first draw a horizontal line perpendicular to the grain arrow. Remember that on this exercise and most of the ones to follow, we are using the pattern front with the facing folded out of the way on the <u>CF</u>, <u>not</u> <u>on</u> <u>the</u> <u>foldline</u>. Also remember that because we will slash, this is a paper pattern tracing, not the Pellon basic.

Then draw vertical lines every place you want the creased edges of a pleat to occur. Slash the verticals and arrange the pieces on a mounting sheet of paper, lining up the horizontal first line you drew with a yardstick ...both to achieve a straight line and for measuring spaces.

Separate, leaving 2" spaces between each pattern piece for the finished 1" pleat. Tape everything in place and rather than taking time to fold up the paper pleats to figure out the proper "jut" shape each pleat would have at shoulder and neck ends, cut paper in little circular shapes as dotted lines show to later perfect in the fabric after stitching and pressing. Since the bottom hem line is already a straight line, this will not be a concern here.

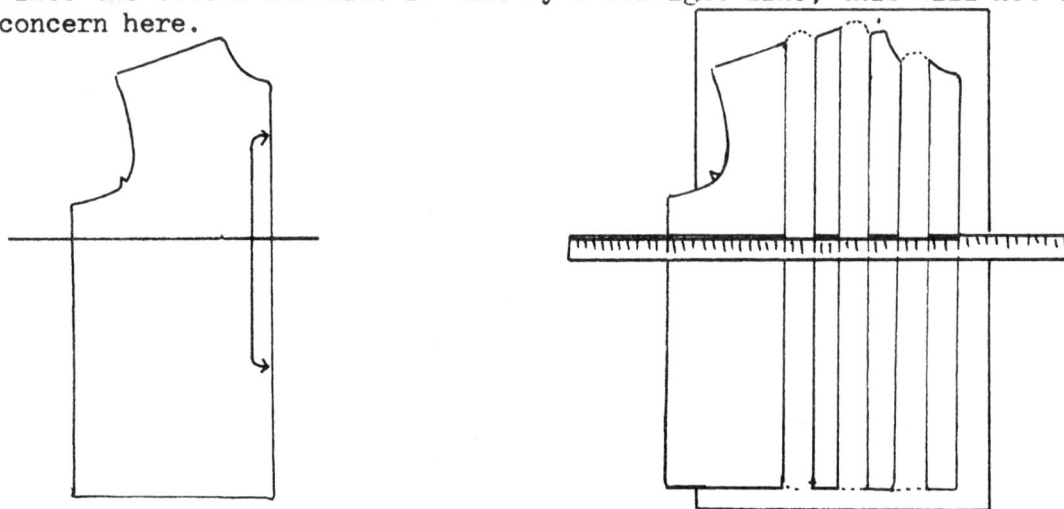

When cutting out fabric, make a tiny clip at each side and on both ends of all the pleats as illustrated. This is a lot quicker and more accurate process to indicate pleat stitching lines than actually marking their entire length with carbon and tracing wheel or by any other method.

On the ironing board fold the pleats one at a time (blouse left and right layers in two separate operations) so that the two clips (which will form the stitching line of a pleat) are together. Pressing this crease is easier if pins hold the folded fabric tautly to the ironing board as shown.

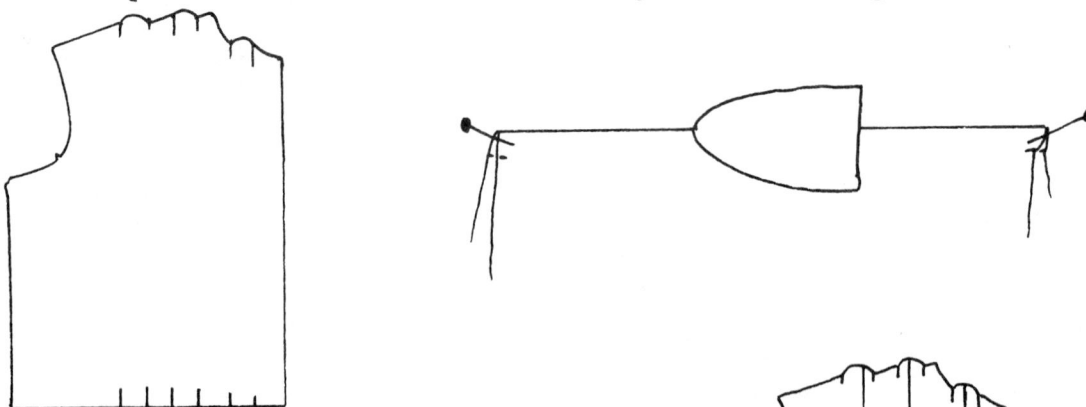

When that crease is pressed, remove pins and repeat the process on each of the other pleats. The completed blouse front looks like this when all pleats are pressed.

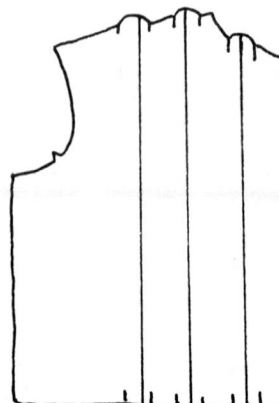

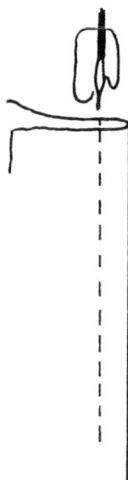

Later, when machine stitching, place each creased pleat on your machine bed lining up the needle and presser foot with the clips, the crease with the 1" marking gauge on your machine.

If your machine lacks such a gauge, secure a piece of masking tape on the machine bed to serve as this gauge. Straight stitching can then be done accurately without tedious individual marking.

If only partially stitched tucks will be used with fullness released at lower ends as shown here, the method is similar but make fabric clips only in top edge, marking lower ends with pins. Or mark little dots with fabric pens whose markings later disappear.

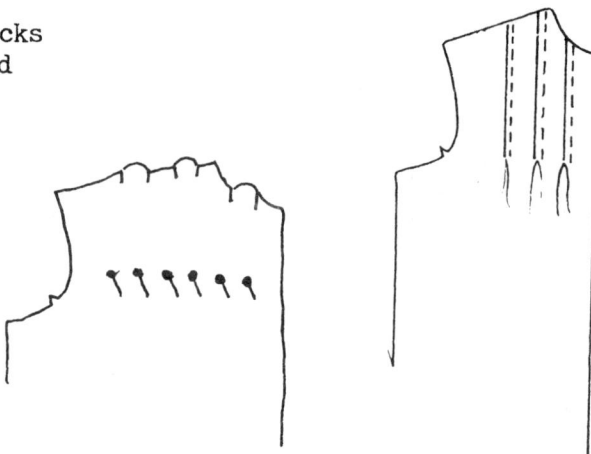

The pressing-to-crease, and machine stitching techniques are the same as previously illustrated.

Points to remember in making the pattern for these stitched pleats or tucks are: 1. Draw the horizontal line on pattern before any slashing is done for proper placement of pieces later when spreading and securing to mounting paper.
2. Slash vertically each place where a pleat is desired.

3. Spread pattern pieces <u>twice</u> the width of the finished tuck. ie: a $\frac{1}{4}$" tuck is spread $\frac{1}{2}$". A $\frac{1}{2}$" tuck is spread 1", etc.

<u>Horizontal</u> <u>tucks</u>. Horizontal tucks are also possible and done the same way you learned for vertical tucks.

Slash the pattern everywhere you want a tuck to occur and spread if twice the width of the desired finished tuck. Clip markings, crease with iron, stitch and press.

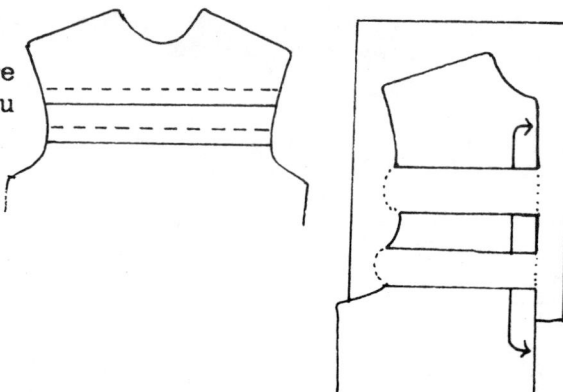

PLEAT FIRST, THEN CUT OUT

This is the easiest way to make a pleated or tucked garment with untucked pattern.

1. Cut a length of fabric which measures the blouse pattern length.

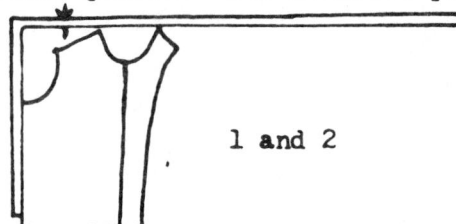

2. Lay pattern on fabric and scissor clip at top where pleats will begin. ↓

3. Pin in two pleats the size and distance apart desired. Clip the outer fold of pleats.

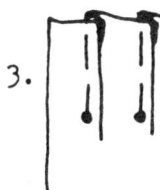

4. Remove pins and with seam gauge measure distance between pleats.

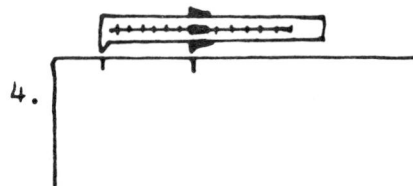

5. Fold up bottom edge of fabric and continue 1/4" scissor clips through top and bottom fabric edges for as many pleats as will be made.

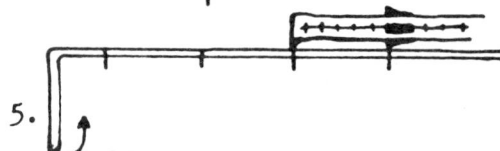

6. On ironing board stretch out matching clips top and bottom, pin to board padding and crease with iron.

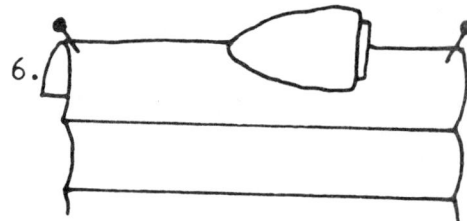

7. Stitch desired pleat width using gauge on sewing machine throat plate at each crease.

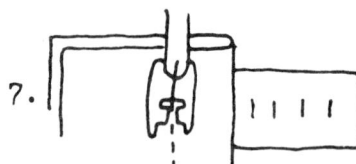

8. On ironing board press all pleats flat.

9. Pin basic pattern on pleated fabric and cut out.

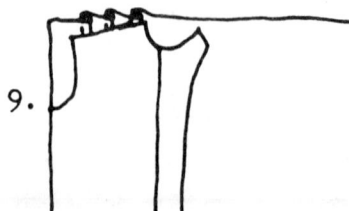

Double-needle pintucking is another version of this. On the rectangle of flat fabric (no pressing of creases necessary) use a twin needle and two spools of thread to make multiple rows of 1/16" pintucks before cutting out with pattern.

Bibs. This tucking may also be done on
bibs, the bib cut any width and length
you want.

In front of a mirror, hold the pattern
front up to yourself and determine
where the line shall be. Draw it
on the paper and hashmark across
bib and blouse, marks later to
be converted to notches.

To both these pieces, 5/8" seam
allowances must be added at cut
edges. Then slash for pleats
whichever section you want pleated.

If a lot of 1/8" pintucks will be
used throughout the bib, it is
easier to first tuck a rectangular
piece of fabric which is slightly
larger than the finished bib will
be. Cut out the bib with its
pattern after the tucking is finished.

This bib technique is also good for
utilizing the drama of striped
fabric, or contrast of colors.

See end of book for the technique
of stitching an inside and an outside curve together.

   If accenting the edge of this bib
with piping would appeal to you, also in
that back section can be found these directions.

   The past many examples have been
shown cut on the CF fold, but could
just as easily have a band added
for front buttoning.

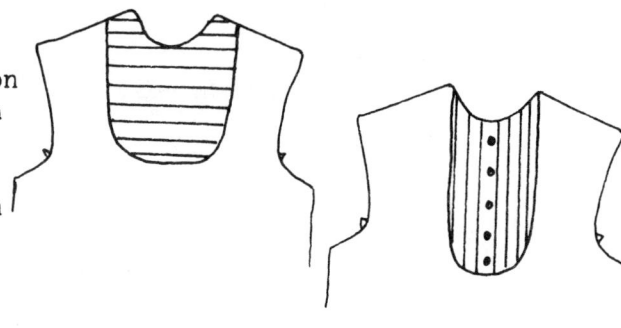

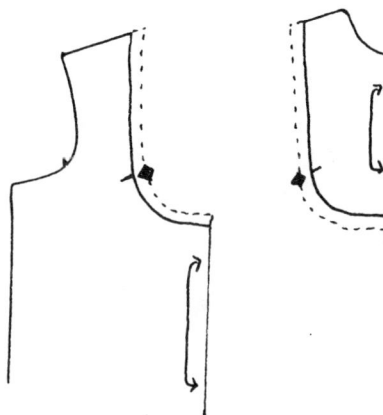

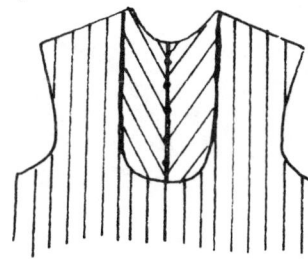

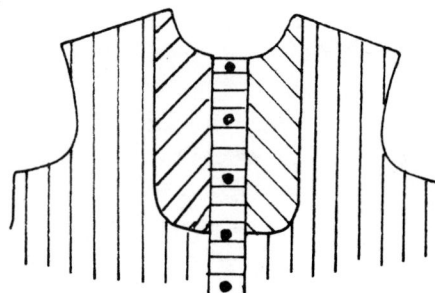

Diagonal tucks can be made the same way as previously described but be sure to pleat with the grain of the fabric. To pleat the fabric on the bias would result in unsightly pulls and ripples.

After pleats are stitched and pressed, then lay the pattern on the fabric bias to cut out.

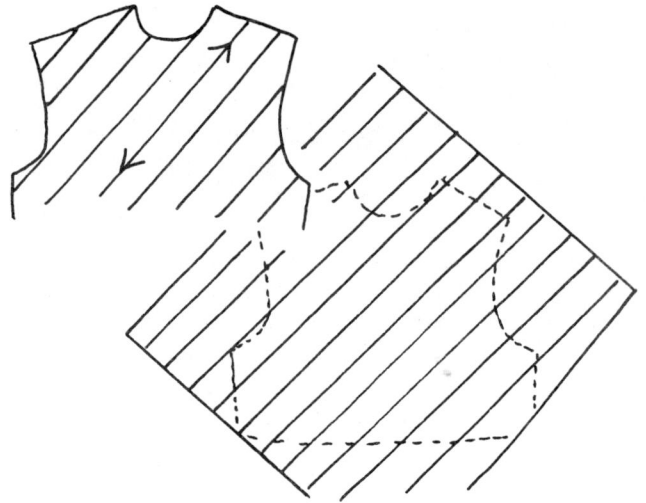

Harlequin pintucking is another version of this where the fabric is first tucked on the straight grain one direction, then turned and repeated in the perpendicular direction. For this the fabric is not creased, but stitched out flat with a twin needle and two top spools of thread producing the tiny tucks. Any machine which is capable of zigzag stitching can do this. It is merely straight stitching but because of the width of the two needles, a wider hole in the throat plate is needed as would be found on zigzag machines. These needles are available in different widths and the more widely spaced they are, the deeper each tuck will be from about 1/16" to 1/4".

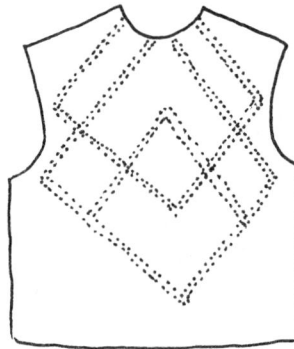

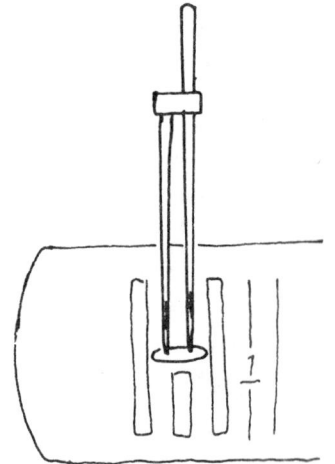

Pulling threads is still another embellishment for a plain fabric such as a linen. On a square of fabric large enough for the pattern piece to be used, pull a few yarns out of the fabric in each space of designated intervals from the cut edges.

After desired effect is achieved, stitch each blank edge with a line of stretch stitching, set in a zigzag width, to secure fabric yarns in place. This produces a very attractive, unique appearance on that plain fabric looking somewhat like faggoting.

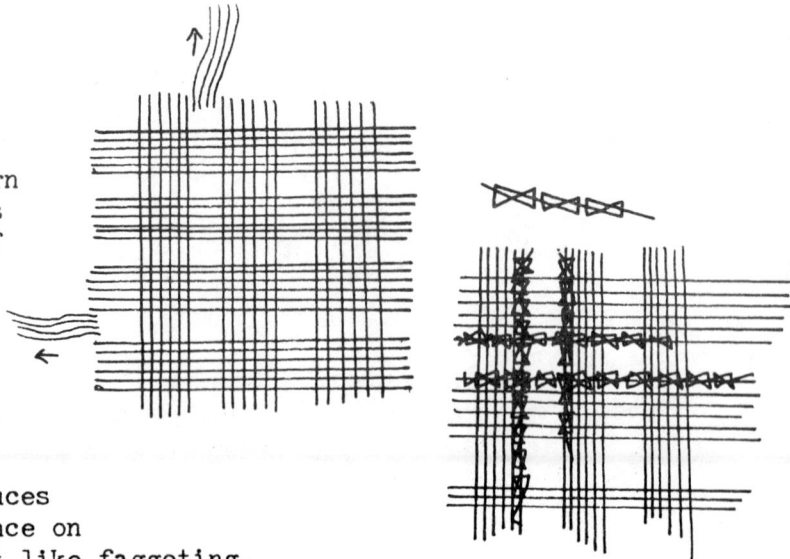

Sunburst tucks or gathers. The tucks
so far shown were parallel. Another
possibility is to have them in a
sunburst arrangement.

The pattern would be slashed
and spread as illustrated. Cut to,
but not through, the pattern edge
to which each points. Then spread
open the desired amount and tape
to a mounting paper or tape strips
in each opening.

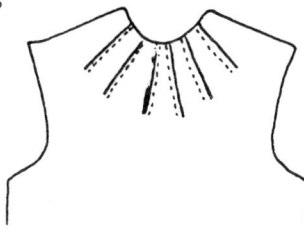

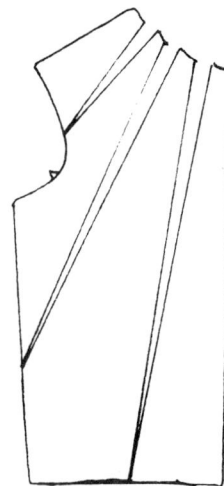

Do not use a soft fabric
for this or tucks will ripple
because of the bias angles. A
crisp fabric would be more successful.

This very same design could
be gathered at the neck instead
of stitching down the tucks. Either
a facing cut from the original
pattern (not cut from the slashed
and spread neckline) or a bias
binding, or a collar could then
secure the gathers in place at
the neck.

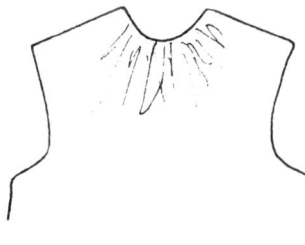

Notice how on this design that
extra fullness occurs only where the
pattern is spread open. The lower hem
is therefore, no fuller than on the
original pattern.

If you want the whole front
fuller because of the gathers, do
it this way using the "move-it-over"
technique without bothering to slash
the pattern.

Place the pattern on the fabric
to be cut out with the CF away from
the fold half as much as you desire
in extra fullness. Ex.: If placed
2" from fold, 4" of extra front
fullness will result. This example
has the fullness the entire length
of the blouse front and gathers would
be only at CF area, not out on shoulders.

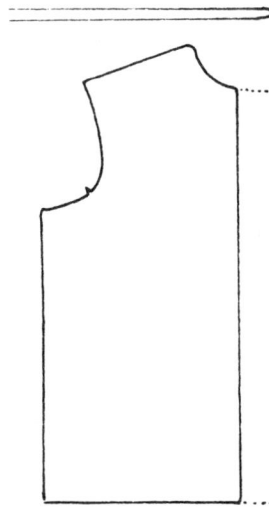

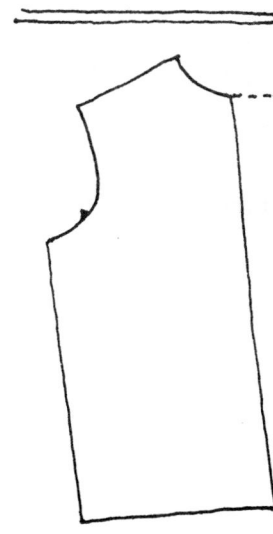

If no excess width is wanted at hemline,
add only at neck by tilting the pattern on the
fabric fold.

Shoulder gathering. To add fullness and
have gathered shoulders held only by the
back shoulder seam as illustrated is a
poor idea because it spreads out awkwardly
at front sleeve cap. There are ways to
control this. Let's first do a novelty
treatment.

It is possible to cut both front
and back bodice with extra width for
later gathering. One way is to slash
and spread, trueing shoulder seam with
a straight edge connecting sleeve and
neck points as shown.✗

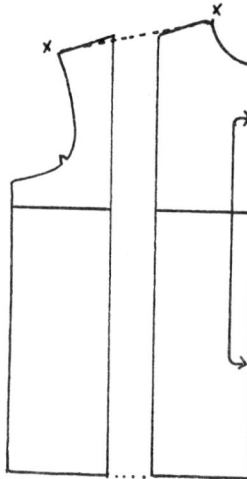

The same thing can be accomplished
by using the move-it-over technique,
cutting from CF over to mid-shoulder,
moving pattern out sideways a few inches,
and continue cutting rest of shoulder,
armscye and side seam. Both these
methods add fullness throughout the
blouse's length.

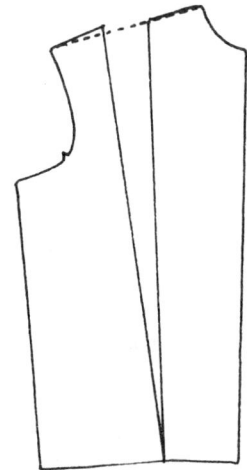

Another alternative if no
extra fullness is desired at hem,
is to slash through shoulder down to,
but not through, lower hem and
fan out.

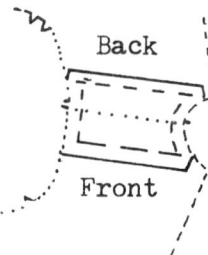

Then an epaulet would be needed
to control this fullness and hold it
in place. This epaulet piece would be
cut the length of the shoulder seam
from neck to sleeve by overlapping the
original pattern back and front at their
shoulder stitching lines as shown. The
epaulet would be as wide as you desire it
to extend into front and back plus the
turn-under seam allowances.

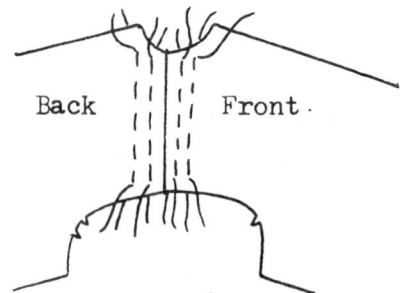

Seam the front and back blouse
shoulders together and press seam open.
Run gathering stitches as shown.

Press under the front and back 5/8"
seams of epaulet leaving the neck and sleeve
edges of it out straight. Gather up the blouse
until it fits the epaulet. Pin and top-stitch
it in place.

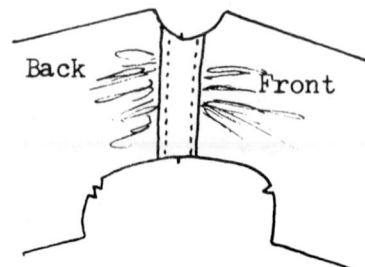

Back

Front

Back   Front

Back   Front

23

Gathers controlled by front yoke.

The most usual way to treat front shoulder gathers is by utilizing a small yoke to hold gathers in place.

Begin by drawing a yoke line on the front shoulder wherever you want it... usually 1½" - 2" below the shoulder stitching line. Cut off and add seams to both cut edges.

Tape that cut-off front piece to the blouse back pattern overlapping the seams so the stitching lines coincide.

Now instead of a shoulder seam, the back continues into the front for a yoke seam. It is wise to put a tiny clip in the fabric armscye where the old shoulder used to be to match up sleeve cap dot to it later.

Separate yokes. Any longer yoke than the previous example would not be combined with the back, but would keep its shoulder seam.

Any of the yokes pictured are done in the same manner:
1. In a mirror determine desired yoke line and draw on pattern. Hashmark.
2. Cut at yoke line, add seam allowances and notches to both parts.
3. Add gathers, pleats, etc. (if desired) to appropriate part.

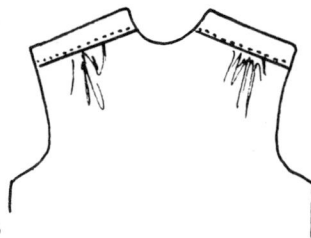

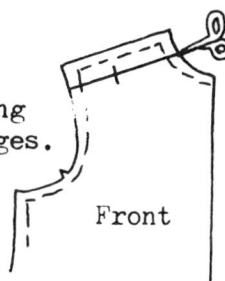

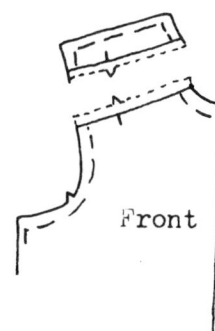

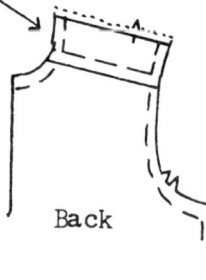

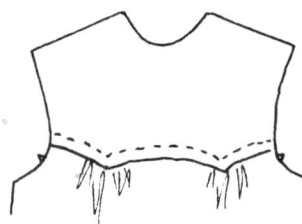

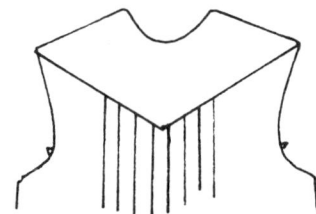

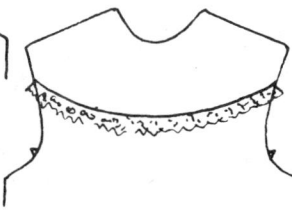

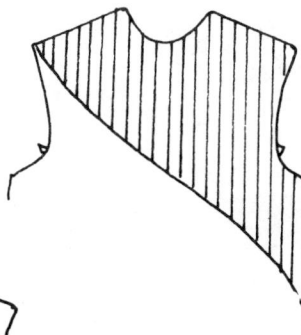

Front

Front

Back

Assymetrical designs are possible if an entire front pattern is used and slashed.

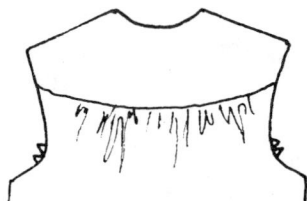

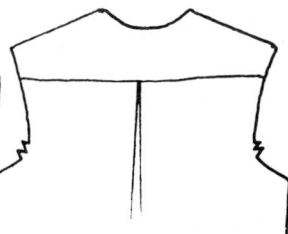

The blouse back is done in the same way as techniques learned on the front.

Assymetrical <u>drapes</u> also need two pattern fronts taped together. Draw slash lines where fabric draping is desired. <u>Do</u> <u>not</u> make them too close to the neck, pointing to the opposite armscye, as this is too high and produces ungraceful draping. Instead, angle top slash to side seam.

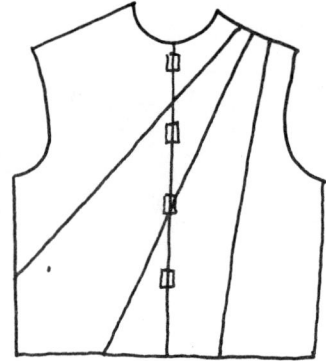

Open each slash <u>twice</u> the width of the finished pleats. Mount the slashed pattern on a backing paper and pleat the shoulder in place. While in this folded position, cut off excess paper at cutting line so that the correct "jut" results for each pleat. The center front line from neck to hem usually becomes the grain line to lay on the straight of fabric, making the pleats pull in softly bias direction.

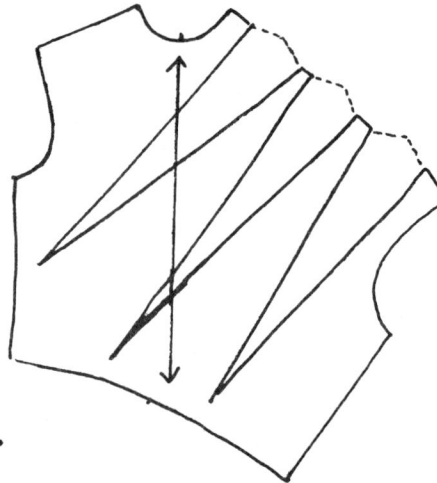

This shoulder could also be gathered in place instead of pleating.

<u>Additional</u> <u>details</u>...<u>pockets</u>.
Remember that upper pockets will only be decorative, not functional, so they needn't be large enough to put your hand in. They only need to be in scale to the blouse part where used and look as though they belong.

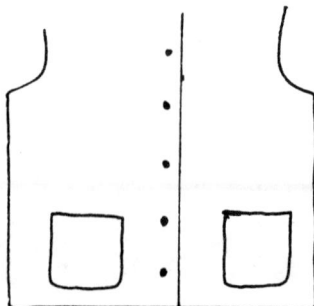

If pockets will be used in the lower part of a blouse, more than likely it will be worn out as a jacket rather than tucked in. These pockets would need to be large enough for the hand to fit.

Only a small time investment, a pocket can add a distinctive touch to an otherwise plain blouse. Even though your pattern doesn't include them in plans, it's relatively easy to add them. Following are directions for a couple of types you may want to consider.

PATCH POCKETS of any shape are very easy. Determine their size and shape according to whether they will be functional or strictly decorative. If their placement will be up in the bust area, hands will never go in them. They therefore may be smaller than those placed lower which will actually be used. Cut a paper pattern of pleasing proportions adding seam allowances and a top foldover hem. If more firmness is needed, interface backside of foldover hem.

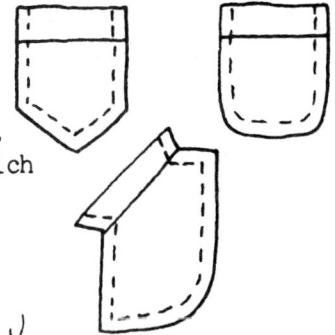

To construct in fabric, finish top edge, fold top hem down right sides together and stitch sides on 5/8" seam lines. Trim off part of seam allowance in foldover.

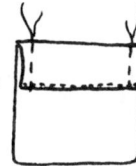

Turn right side out and press, also pressing under remaining seam allowances. Pin to garment and try on to be sure placement on body is correct before topstitching in place.

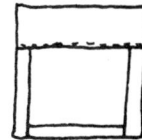

BUTTONHOLE POCKET may be designed vertically, horizontally, or diagonally according to desired look, location, and function.

If the fabric is ravelly, or needs extra reinforcement to "beef it up" or take strain away...press a strip of fusible light weight interfacing to garment backside of stitching area where pocket will be placed.

Cut a bias strip of fashion fabric twice the length of pocket opening plus 2½" long, and 1" or so wide. This may be corded with yarn or thin cording for extra weight and stability. Use zipper-cording foot to stitch close to cord.

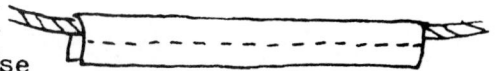

Cut strip in half and pin them in position on right side of garment, raw edges together. Machine baste in place.

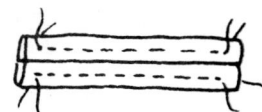

fold of fabric

From fashion fabric cut a pocket desired size on fold, plus seam allowances.

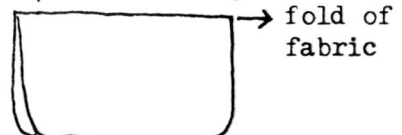

Position pocket (right side of fabric out)
over strips with fold at center. Flip top half
up and pin ends through all layers. Additional
pins at upper and lower edges keep layers in place
when they are hidden from view.

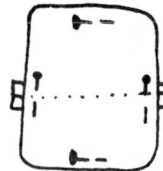

With wrong side of garment up stitch (small
stitches, backstitching either end) retracing former
machine basting lines.

Pocket side up, slash on center fold line
cutting <u>pocket</u> <u>layer</u> <u>only</u> all the way across.

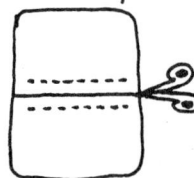

Garment side up, cut through <u>garment</u> <u>layer</u>
<u>only</u> midway between stitching lines and
diagonally out to corners.

Turn pocket and strip ends through to wrong
side of garment. Fold edges of strips automatically
turn to center. Holding garment up out of the way,
stitch corner diagonals, strips, and pocket
edges together. Press.

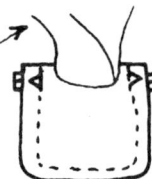

An <u>in-seam</u> <u>pocket</u> is a nice design
feature added in a small version if
above bust area strictly as a design,
or if placed lower in an overblouse
it will need to be large enough for your hand.

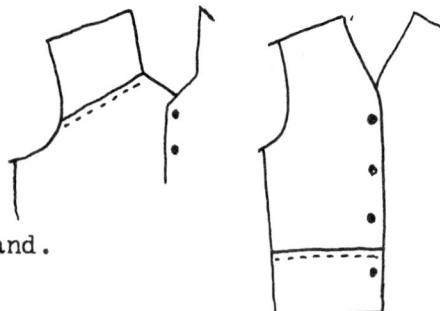

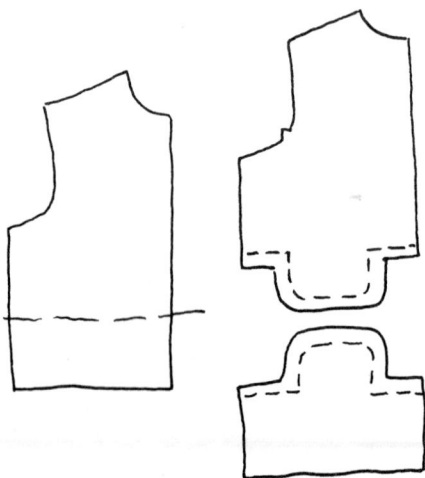

Cut the pattern piece
apart at whatever level and whatever angle is
desired. To the cut edges add seam allowances
and pocket shapes as illustrated, making sure
the two pockets are duplicates of each other
so they later will match up for stitching.

Stitch edges together,
press seams and pocket
in the down direction.

Extra "flying" layers, seen in
some fashion periods on either
bodice back or front, are simply
partial repeats of the basic pieces.

Tracing the original pattern
in area desired, cut off at whatever
length seems most flattering.

In the fabric finish the loose
edges with a topstitched rolled hem.
Staystitch neck, shoulder and armscye
edges to base fabric, then handle as
one piece while completing the blouse.

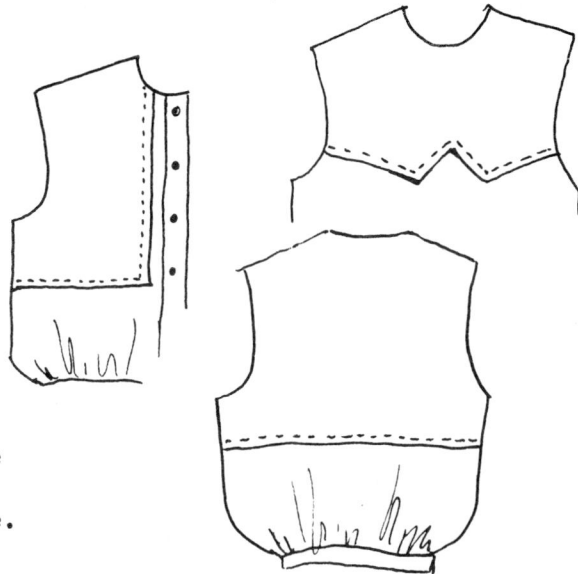

Shoulder epaulets are simple little
additions easily made. Cut two layers
of fabric about 2 1/2" wide including
the seam allowances.

The length should be twice your
shoulder length, with one end tapered.
Stitch layers together leaving straight
end open. Turn, press, topstitch edge
(optional) and make a machine buttonhole.

Staystitch end at neck of blouse.
Stitch fold point x out at sleeve cap
seam, sew on button in appropriate spot.
Fold end over and button in place.

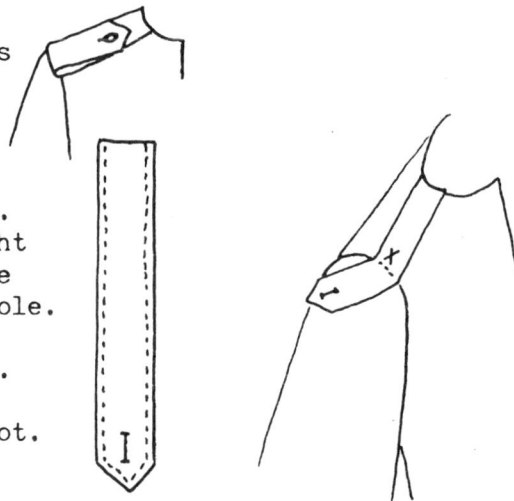

Shoulder pads. A pattern which plans
for shoulder pads will have excess
height added on shoulder out towards
armscye. If your pattern hasn't
included this space, with a ruler
taper a straight line from nothing
at the neck edge up to 1/4" extra
above armscye edge. This will be
needed on both back and front pattern
pieces. The sleeve cap will also
need a little more heighth.

Directions for making shoulder
pads are in the last section of this
book.

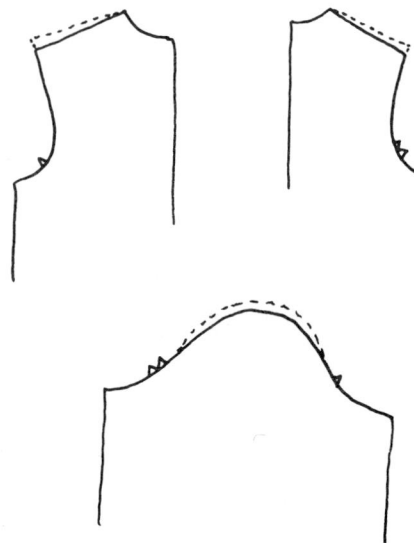

Lace or eyelet insertions.
     When these are used, often it is
bordering a front band. In which case,
one edge of the lace is sewn into the
band seam. If there is a scalloped or
decorative edge, that edge may be topstitched to the blouse layer. Think whether
that raw edge should be finished to prevent
raveling before topstitching the lace in
place. If a decorative edge is not used,
it may just be a regular narrow seam in
attaching. For this "see-through" look,
remember to cut away the part of the blouse
pattern which the lace will replace. If
opaqueness is more desirable, topstitch
lace over fabric rather than cutting it out.

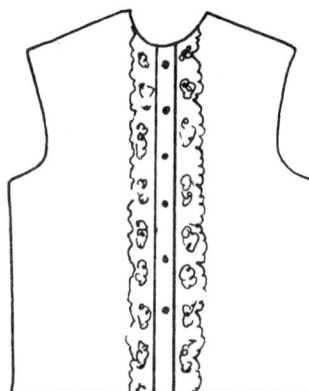

Ruffles and flounces. Analyze the ruffles
you see in ready-to-wear blouses and notice
the different techniques they have used.

     If it looks like this cascading
gracefully in folds at its loose edge
with no gathering where attached, it
was cut in a circular shape. The outer
edge has a tiny rolled hem and the inner
edge of the circle is stitched into a seam. The inner edge must measure
the length of the area where it will be sewn at the stitching line, not
out at the cut edge. Circular pieces can be seamed together to produce
greater length. Tiny clips must be made in the inner seam allowance to
stitch into the seam smoothly without puckers or pleats.

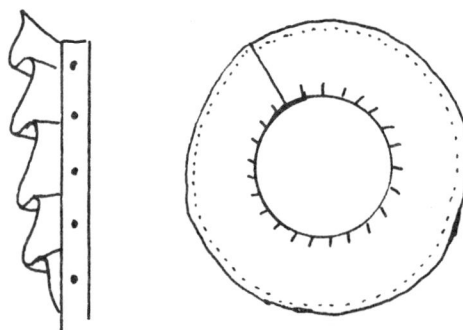

     If the fabric is quite sheer, it might be better to cut double and
seam the two thicknesses together on the outer curve rather than roll
hemming it. They would then be turned and pressed before attaching it
to the blouse.

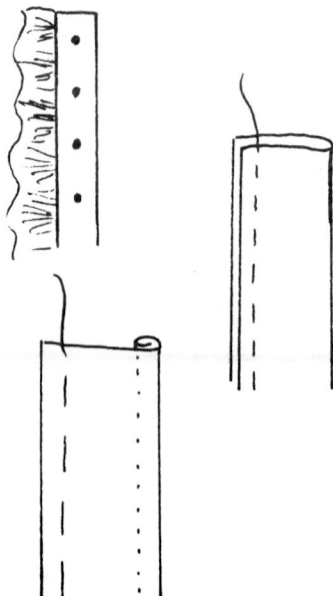

If gathers appear where stitched in,
it was cut in a straight line and gathered
into place before attaching. If the fabric
is very soft this strip may be cut on the
straight. If more softness is desired,
it should be bias cut.

If the fabric is very thin, it is
sometimes cut double, pressed in half
before gathering the two layers together.
The outside fold substitutes for a hem.

If this would be too heavy, a little
rolled hem is necessary either by hand or
by machine. The time to hem this is while
the strip is still flat, before it is
gathered up.

Combining pattern pieces is a possibility when
it is advantageous to eliminate a seam. A typical
situation would be avoiding breaking up a large
fabric print, or for continuity of horizontal pleats
all around the body of a blouse.

   Overlap the side seams of back and front at
the stitching lines and cut the entire bodice as
one piece. In order to make the center back and
center front grainlines parallel, it may be necessary
to slightly change the side seam angles.

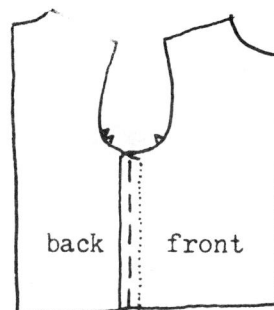

back   front

Overblouse waistband. Cut blouse shorter
at lower edge, not exactly at waistline
marking, but a couple of inches below to
allow for blousing. This is later
gathered into a fitted waistband.

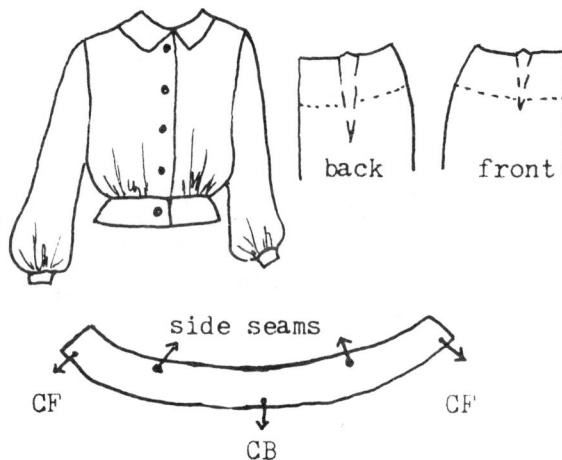

back   front

   The waistband may be cut in a straight
strip. It is probably easier to wear
however, if this band is shaped. Use
for this the top 2" or 3" of a skirt
pattern whose side seams are overlapped
and darts folded out. The finished band
would be curved to better fit the upper
hip area.

side seams

CF   CF

CB

Dresses. A blouse needn't stay in its abbreviated form to be worn with
skirt or pants. Just extend the vertical seams down long enough to make
it a dress. Note:
   1. Length should include some blousing at the waist, plus skirt length,
      plus lower hem.
   2. Make sure its width is sufficient for the hip area. It may be
      necessary to widen as explained at first of book in pattern fitting
      section.

   When doing this, it is fine to complete the blouse-grown-into-a-
dress including its hem which you make straight all around. The hem shouldn't
vary in width one place to another, because any dress, skirt or pants should
actually hang from the waist, not be regulated in the hem. It is therefore,
at the waist where adjustments are made if it will be worn belted. No
guarantees for straightness when unbelted!

   Personal feelings are that it is most annoying to have a one-piece
dress (without a waistline seam) shift around each time one sits...necessitating
adjustment so it hangs right when you stand back up. How often is there a
mirror handy to do this in? To avoid the problem, elasticize the waist and
it will always stay in place beautifully.

For perfection in the way it hangs, put on the completed dress and pin elastic snugly over it at the waist. In front of a full length mirror or with the help of a friend, adjust the dress above the elastic blousing more here, less there, until it hangs exactly straight at the hem. Watch also that its hem extends equal amounts from your legs...side to side, and front to back. When perfect, mark dress fabric at lower edge of elastic with fabric marker little dots all around as this is your exact waistline. Use the type fabric marker which can be removed later at the touch of a damp cloth or the type which automatically disappears after a day or so. If you lack these, have a friend mark with a row of straight pins.

Then take the dress off but wear the elastic around the house over skin or a slip for a couple of hours to make sure it will be comfortable. If too tight, time can produce misery and better to discover it now before attaching it to the dress. You are permitted to wear clothes over the elastic for this trial period! If the size is correct, mark elastic where it overlaps before removing.

Machine stitch that overlap so the elastic is in the permanent circle. This method is only used when planning to zigzag directly to the inside of the dress where the waist is marked. (Transpose those exterior markings to the inside of the dress). This may be done if the elastic will stretch out the size of the dress waist, to be pinned in place at regular intervals before stitching.

If it will not stretch out large enough for direct stitching, sew a casing to the inside of the dress at waist markings, and later insert the elastic through it before joining elastic ends.

NECKLINES

Let's move on to deal with the blouse neckline. The standard basic blouse pattern has a high round neckline located at the neck base. This may be used as is without a collar, as was shown in all the pattern examples thus far illustrated. It is usually called a jewel neckline.

To reshape this, work in front of a mirror with a piece of yarn or string varying its length and shape until you discover what you like. From the original neckline (X mark and usually in the hollow spot between bone structure), measure down how far the new neckline will be and duplicate that measurement on your pattern front.

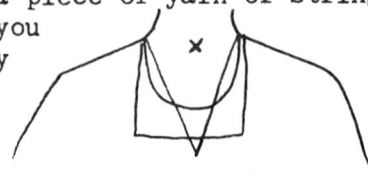

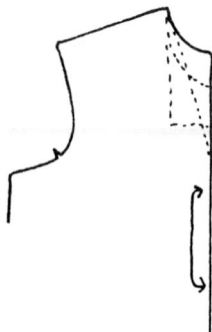

Square, low round, vee...whatever you like is usually changed only in front and the shoulder-neck point is where the change begins.

To make the front facing for any of these, the process is as explained earlier in book...a duplicate of the outside fabric at neckline cutting it as wide as seems appropriate.

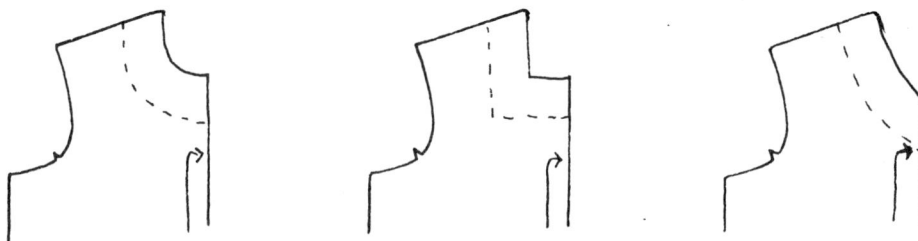

When lowered necklines gap as they might, especially with a hollow chest area, a stay may be necessary to pull it in more tightly. If the shape is V or round, there is a lot of bias edge which can stretch out unless carefully handled to prevent it. The bias also enables easing it in without obvious puckers. This stay is a strip of fabric, thin, narrow, non-stretch which will stabilize and "stay" the area in place. You might use for this a 1/4" twill tape, purchased by the yard or in a 3-yard package. Black or white are the only choices for this. Another possibility is hem tape or seam tape (NOT bias tape as no stretch is wanted) which includes a large variety of color choices.

Apply this stay by first pinning to the backside of neckline edge drawing it up as tightly as is necessary to ease neck in place when tried on. Staystitch tape to neckline. After facing is applied the stay will be concealed between layers.

If the neckline will be bias bound instead of faced, stretch the bias strips sufficiently while applying that when they revert to their original size, they will automatically ease edge in smaller. The proper amount to stretch this is difficult to gauge while stitching. Perhaps it would be wise to pin it in place first to be sure it will turn out just right.

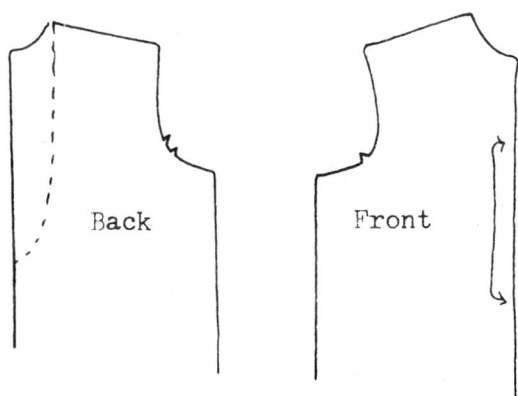

Back   Front

It is certainly possible to also lower the back and sides of a neckline and here again...try the yarn on your body to determine what pleases you.

When lowering the back, it stays on the body in place more easily if neck front is left high. When everything is lowered it slips off the shoulders with every body motion and may be uncomfortable to wear.

Bateau or boat. Although this comes out wider
on the shoulders, the front and back neck are
usually higher than the basic because it forms
a straight horizontal line perpendicular to
the CF and CB.

This is how the pattern is changed...
raised at CF and CB enough to form that
horizontal line. This has no button
opening and is just slipped over the head.

Begin by putting a tape measure around
your head, holding its overlap in a circle,
and slipping it up and down to be sure it will
work. Note what the measurement is.

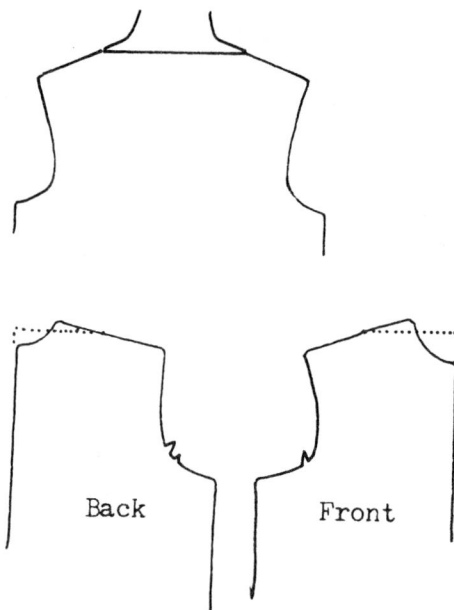

Back   Front

Then be sure the actual blouse neckline is large enough. For example:
Your head needs 22". Give it 23" so it won't be too difficult to slip over.
23" divided by 4 equals 5 3/4". Measure the
center-out-to-shoulder-point X line (usually
same back and front and in fact, must be in
the same place on shoulder back and front so
from that point out to sleeve it will stitch
together) to see if it works.

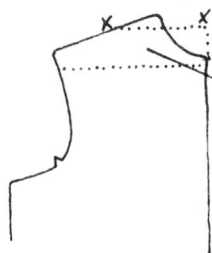

The facing for a bateau often goes out
to the armscye seam as illustrated rather
than just surrounding the neck.

If this width to get it over your
head needs to be so wide it reveals
lingerie straps, curve down slightly
at center front and center back to gain
a little more head space without so much
width. Another alternative is to have
a small button opening at side neck.

Still another idea is using triangular
insets out at shoulder-armscye area. This is
an especially good treatment when a border
print is used needing a straight line across
from shoulder points. The front corner of
one of these insets can remain unstitched
and closed by a snap.

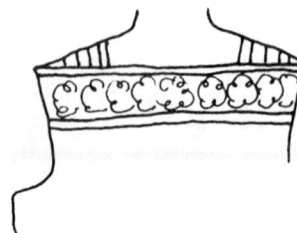

Cowl. Cowl necklines only work when made in soft, drapable fabric. They
are totally unsatisfactory in heavy or stiff fabric and shouldn't be
attempted. The bodice back remains standard as it should be high and
tight to hold the front in place. Cowls are of two types: one or two piece.

One piece, shallow cowl. This features only slight
draping at front near neck. It is achieved by
adding a little more width and heighth at center
front.

    The simplest way to do this is to place
the CF pattern not right on the fold of the
fabric to cut out, but to pivot slightly so
lower edge touches, top is away.

    In addition, cut a little higher at
CF tapering to original at neck-shoulder
point.

Deep cowl is accomplished by slash and the
draping extends down lower into blouse because
more width is added there...how much depending
on how far slashes are opened up.

    By making the neck a straight line
perpendicular to CF (a wise choice),
a cut-on facing can be utilized and just
folded down into place without the
necessity of any extra seams which
could stiffen it undesirably.

    This could also be done with a cowl
back, but the front should then remain
high and straight to stabilize the back.
Don't attempt to cowl both back and front
as it would too easily fall off the
shoulders making the wearing of it
uncomfortable.

    If done in a crisp fabric,
the result would not be the above
drape. It is possible however,
and could be quite attractive,
appearing as sketched with the
excess fabric falling over to
one side.

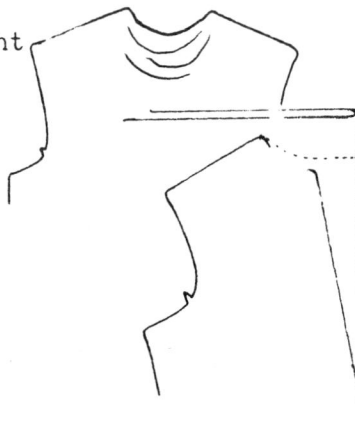

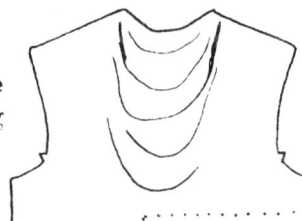

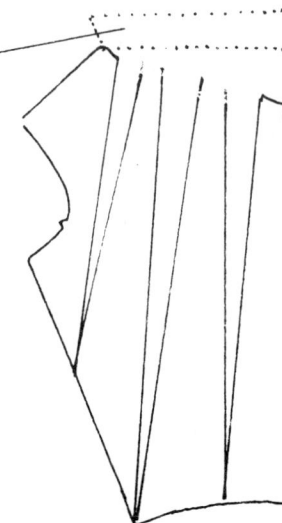

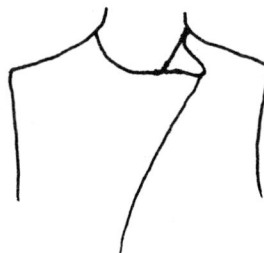

Two-piece cowl. This is done when the blouse or dress is intended to remain more fitted throughout its lower part, only draping up in the cowl section.

First cut out the cowl piece in either a rounded or a V shape.

Add seam allowances to both cut edges, developing notches from hashmark. The lower front is ready to use as is.

Then slash and spread the cowl section only and attach a cut-on neck facing.

COLLARS

Collars can be grouped into three different categories: rolled, fitted or shaped, and bias. Plus there are possibly a few maverick novelties which defy grouping.

Rolled. This is the collar commonly found on coats and suits, men's shirts and probably on your basic blouse. Frequently it is called a tailored or straight collar. There are many variations but its basic pattern looks like this: (this is not a full size)

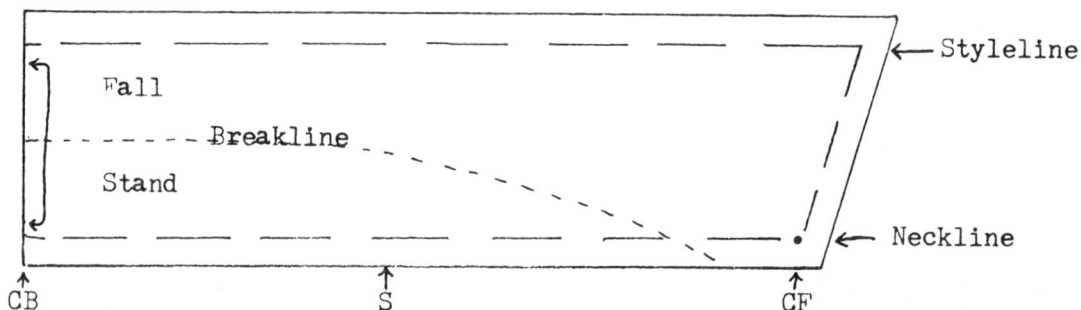

The neckline must be the same size from CB to shoulder to CF as your blouse pattern measures, not at the cutting line, but at the stitching lines. It is sometimes slightly curved, but its length must remain the same in order to fit when stitched to the blouse. The shoulder dot is closer to the CB than the CF because on the blouse, the back neck is higher, the front neck lower...therefore a longer distance from the shoulder.

The outer style line can vary because it is free and not stitched to anything except the second layer of itself. In some fashion periods it extends to long exagerated points at the center front, and at other times it is short and more squared or rounded off.

The stand and fall divided by the breakline occur because its neckline shape is relatively straight instead of round like the blouse neckline it will be stitched to. How high it stands before breaking into the fall depends on how wide you design it at the center back.

To design it without a pattern, stand a tape measure on end and measure the curved distance from CB to shoulder. Do the same from shoulder to CF. That total distance is drawn in a straight line for the collar neckline.

Decide how high you want it to stand at back neck when completed and folded down into place. Multiply that by two (for both stand and fall) and this is the CB width.

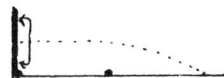

A line parallel to the neckline but slightly extended beyond CF is the style line. Connect it to CF and your pattern only needs the addition of seam allowances to be complete.

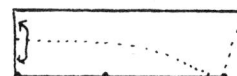

Convertible. The standard rolled collar above stands slightly away from your neck at top fold and if you wear the front neck open (unbuttoned) it lays a little awkwardly. Convertible implies either open or closed and its shape is only a slight change at the CF neckline. It curves up 1/2" or so (all these measure- ments mentioned refer to full size patterns, not to the illustrations) starting at shoulder as illustrated.

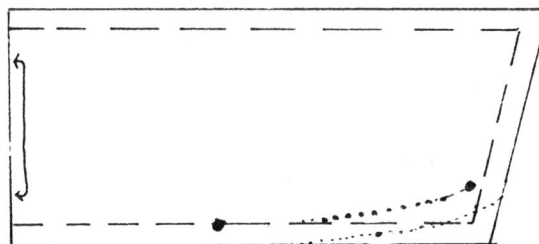

Convertible with button. The former convertible is sometimes reshaped at CF so that it comes out to the edge of the blouse's button extension rather than stopping in the center.

This is done by adding the same 5/8" or 3/4" as is on the blouse front. Dotted lines show this.

Two-piece. Frequently on men's shirts or blouses or dresses the convertible is split into two pieces horizontally, by just drawing the line through it. Hash mark in order to develop notches for stitching it together in the fabric once seam allowances are added to the cut edges.

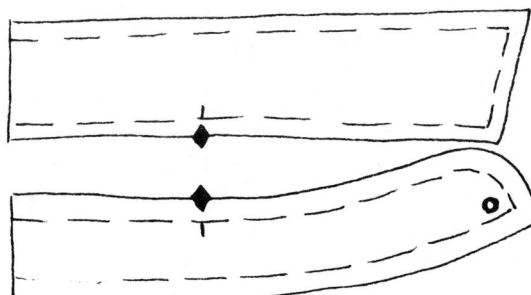

These two pieces are sometimes slightly reshaped where they join.

Mandarin collar. Use the neckline piece
only of the two-piece collar and you have
a lovely stand-up, Nehru, oriental or
mandarin collar whose upper edge gently
shapes into your neck (which is smaller
up higher than at its base).

    If used with its front extension,
it probably would have a button and
buttonhole added. It could also be cut
shorter...back to the CF line and just
meet without buttoning since it would
have no overlap.

Wingtip. To the upper mandarin collar
with the button and buttonhole, add a
wingtip starting at about the shoulder
point. Taper that increasingly wider
as it approaches the center front,
being sure the heighth you add is a
little greater than the heighth of
the original mandarin. This will then
fold down in place like a tuxedo shirt
and its tips extending down a little
below the collar base.

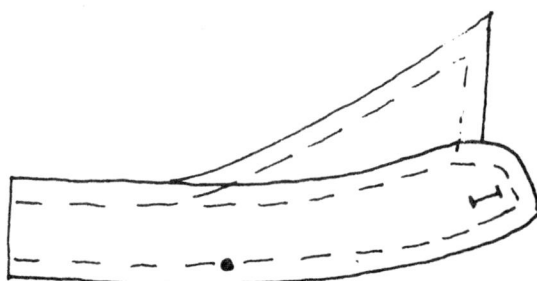

Shawl collar. This is possibly a maverick
but is now being grouped with rolled because
the full-rolled collar is its basis.
Distinguishing marks of a shawl: center
back seam, upper collar and front facing
are cut as one piece, under collar and
blouse front are cut as another piece.

    Place the rolled collar pattern
against the bodice front so the shoulder
dots match up. Notice how shoulder
seam and back neck collar section
form a little less than a right angle.
Collar CF and bodice CF overlap slightly.

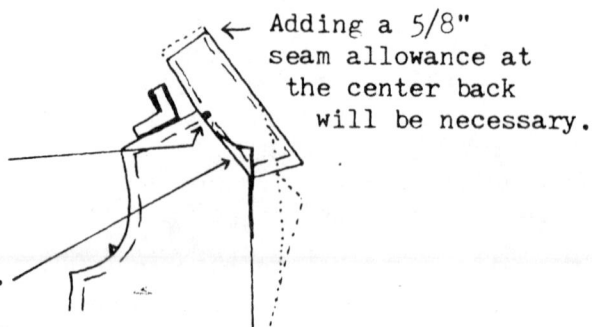

← Adding a 5/8"
   seam allowance at
   the center back
   will be necessary.

    The outer style line can be smoothed
out in a flowing line as sketched above.

Or this style line can be
reshaped into a rounded notched line
or left in the squared off notched line
as the dotted lines indicate.

This pattern becomes the bodice-
undercollar piece. Trace only the front
part of this for the uppercollar-facing
piece.

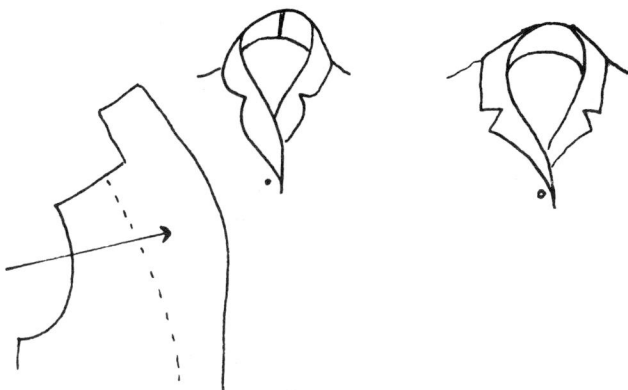

Tie collar is another variation of the rolled collar.
Using the neck measurement, decide by looping a tape
measure how long you want the ties. Be sure to double
the desired width plus seams.

When stitching this tie collar to neckline, stop about 5/8" short
of center front so that there will be space to tie a bow.

Ascot effect tie collar.

Cut this in the aforementioned straight line
at neck, or tapered to a point at ends as desired.
The length would be determined by a tape measure
whose center is placed at the center front of your
neck, crossed over in back, and brought back to
front. Add to that length enough to tie in a
front knot. About 45" would produce a little
single knot. 3" more would be needed for a
square knot.

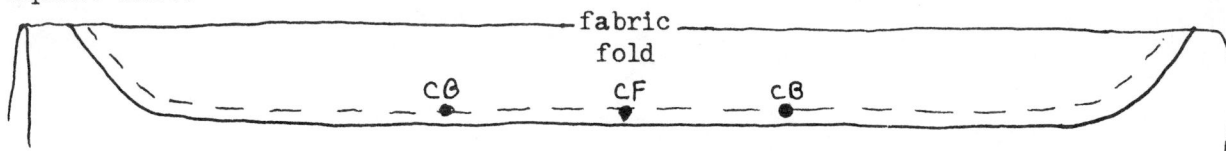

fabric
fold

CB   CF   CB

To tie in a front bow would require still more
length....possibly 65" to 75".

Either of these ascot types will need a
center back opening in the blouse in order to
slip it over your head.

This collar is worn most successfully by someone with a long, slim
neck. A short neck is not flattered by it and would possibly feel
uncomfortably high to the wearer.

Fitted, flat, or shaped collars are the second major category. This is different than the rolled collar because of its neckline shape...round and almost the same as the blouse neck rather than a straight line. Because of this it lies almost flat when stitched into the blouse rather than having a stand and fall. It is therefore sometimes also called round or Peter Pan.

If completely the same shape as blouse neckline, its style line might ripple. To prevent that, shoulders on blouse front and back are slightly overlapped at armscye when making the collar pattern.

This same fitted collar can be small with rounded or pointed front. It can grow bigger and become a bertha or pilgrim collar. Do anything you like with its outer style line and basically, regardless of size, it remains the same collar.

A variation of this is single multi-layers in graduated sizes of a sheer fabric with edge-rolled hems.

Sailor is a variation of the fitted collar but besides being square cut in back, its front is a V neck.

First cut a blouse front to as low a V as desired. Then slightly overlap the front and back shoulders and make your collar in the manner already learned.

Ruffled is another variation of the fitted collar. The outer style line is slashed in several places toward, but not completely through the neck- line, and flared out to produce the ruffle.

Cut two with seam in center back for each layer. After stitching together the back seams, stitch the two layers on outer style line, turn right side out and press.

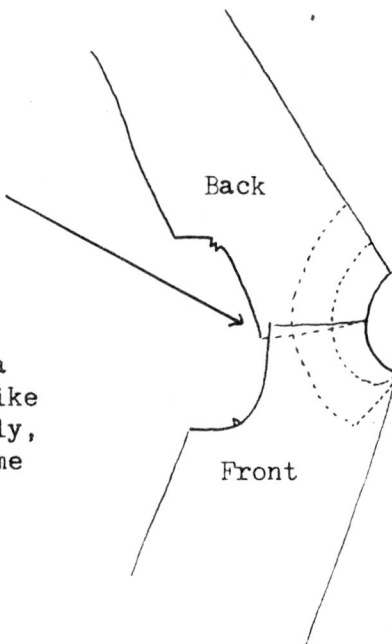

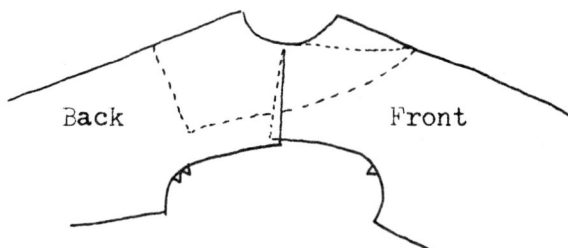

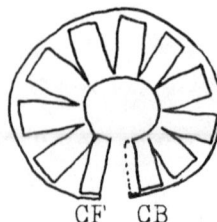

Ruffled collar on a V neck.

Refer to page 30 for the neckline considerations.
Make the inner edge stitching line of the circle
the same measurement as that of the bodice.

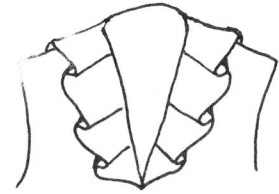

At center front diminish the width to a point.

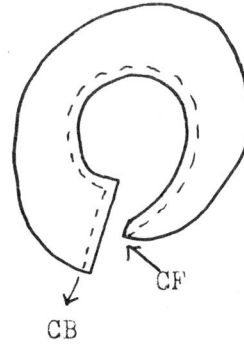

CF

CB

Collars on lowered necklines can be cut
as a flat fitted collar; or if a stand
is wanted in back, as a full roll collar;
or for that matter, even a bias collar.

    The outer style line can be any
shape or size. Just be sure the neck edge
stitching line measures the same as the
bodice neckline.

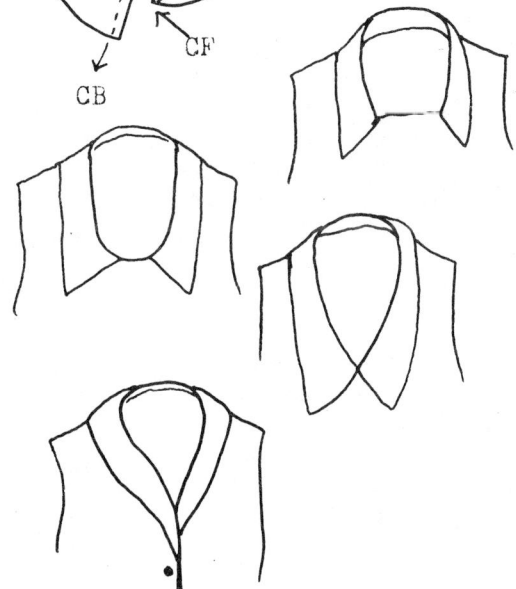

Double layer collars can be made from this fitted
collar (or any collar) and is especially interesting
in a thin, semi-transparent fabric like organdy
or organza. Remember there will need to be
a neckline opening in the blouse where
the collar separates.

    Try it in balanced or assymetrical
shapes. If balanced and both layers are
the same shape, make the upper layer slightly
narrower out at the style line so they both show.

    In the assymetrical sketch one layer is
simply the reverse direction of the other. Its
edge may be a tiny rolled hem. If the
layers would be more appealing cut in
double layers, outer edge seamed, try a
tiny zigzag stitch so seam allowance can
be trimmed very short without fraying.

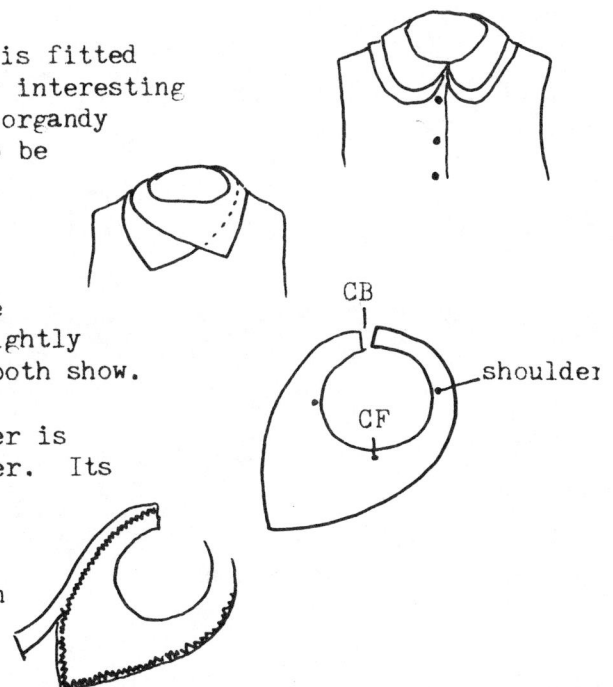

CB

shoulder

CF

Bias collars, the third category, includes tiny fold-over collars or stand-up collars, higher fold-over turtle necks, or wider cowl-neck collars.

Turtle. Same as for the full roll collar, begin with blouse neckline measurement from CB to CF. Make it twice the height you want since it will fold over to hem under and enclose neckline seams on the inside. Four times if you want a second foldover.

If it will be of a woven fabric, cut on the bias so there will be some stretch and so that it will lie more gracefully, softly. In a weave the stretch is insufficient to pull over the head. It will therefore require an opening...zipper or button...at back, front, or on shoulder side.

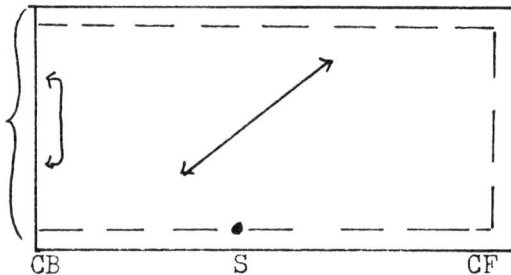

CB   S   CF

In a stretchy knit, such as turtle neck sweaters, an opening is unnecessary. The bias cut also is not used as on a knit, the crosswise stretch is greater.

Cowl. This is the same as a turtle except for the original measurement. It is wider because the blouse neckline has been cut a little lower all around before applying the collar. This makes the measurement bigger in circumference. Otherwise, procedures are the very same.

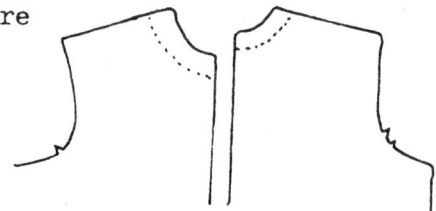

Funnel collars are cut for a slightly lowered neckline, the one illustrated dipping down to a center front point. Referring to the two-piece cowl neck on p. 34, this design may be interpreted as that neckline rather than a collar. The method of making it is similar.

back   front

Add an extension to blouse center back for buttons and buttonholes. Cut down the neckline about an inch and perhaps to a center front point. Remember to later add a seam allowance to blouse neck edge.

Tape together the two cut-off neck pieces at shoulders. Slash upper neck edge in several places and spread out so that it is enlarged somewhere between the original curve and a straight line.

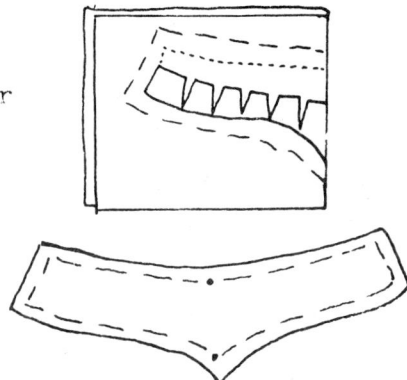

Tape to another paper which is folded at center front. Draw upper edge about 1" higher so it will hit higher on your neck.

Cut the doubled paper out adding a seam allowance to the top, bottom, and end so it will open up to a whole collar pattern. How much to open up the slashes and how much heighth to add is somewhat a trial and error process and may need adjustment. The upper edge should be slightly loose on the neck.

Sashed buttonhole collar may be cut on the bias or straight. Make its length the neck measurement plus about 8" to 12" to loop through the buttonhole and hang free. The end with a large buttonhole will diminish to a point where it attaches to the blouse neckline.

The upper edge between CF markings will be stitched to the blouse neckline. The remaining will be turned wrong side out to be seamed together before turning and pressing.

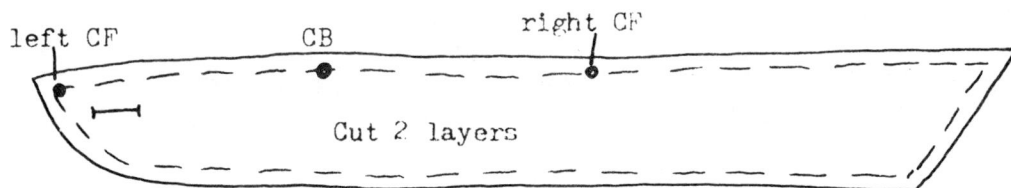

left CF   CB   right CF

Cut 2 layers

SLEEVES

There are basically three types of sleeves:

Set-in   Raglan   Kimono

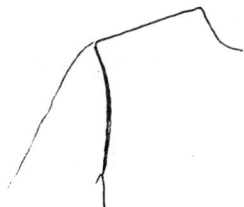 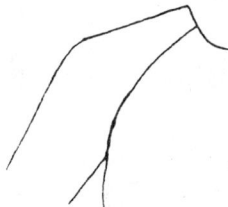 

The set-in sleeve is the standard. It is attached to bodice at the point where arm meets shoulder. The raglan seam comes from underarm and extends up to neck. The kimono has bodice front and sleeve front cut in one piece, bodice back and sleeve back cut in another piece.

The cap seamline measurement is slightly larger than the bodice armscye into which it will be sewn. For this reason the upper cap between the notches is always eased into the armscye. If working with a fabric which will not ease without showing puckers, cut cap slightly smaller to eliminate that ease.

My personal preference in a standard blouse sleeve is to have the vertical sides (seamlines) of the sleeve running parallel to each other. If a sleeve is cut narrower, I prefer to enlarge at the wrist to make them parallel. It is not a good idea to merely add on to the paper pattern as the dotted lines indicate.

The sleeve hangs more gracefully if instead it is slashed up the center and fanned out until the seams are parallel as this continues extra width up into the cap.

Elasticized wrist. If a cuff or sleeveband will not be used but instead replaced by a casing with elastic, add extra length...approximately 2 1/2"...for that casing. and cut lower edge in a straight line for easier turning.

When stitching the fabric, press under 1/4", then press up again 3/4" and stitch in place before inserting elastic. This uses up 1" of the amount added. The rest is needed to replace the eliminated cuff width.

Horizontal tucks. If decorative tucks are desired, additional length is needed. Figure how deep each tuck will be times two. (Ex.: for a 1/4" stitched tuck, add 1/2" in length)

Multiply this by the number of tucks to be made. In the sketched sleeve 1 1/2" additional length is needed (1/2" of length times three tucks). Stitch these in place while sleeve is flat, before vertical seam is stitched.

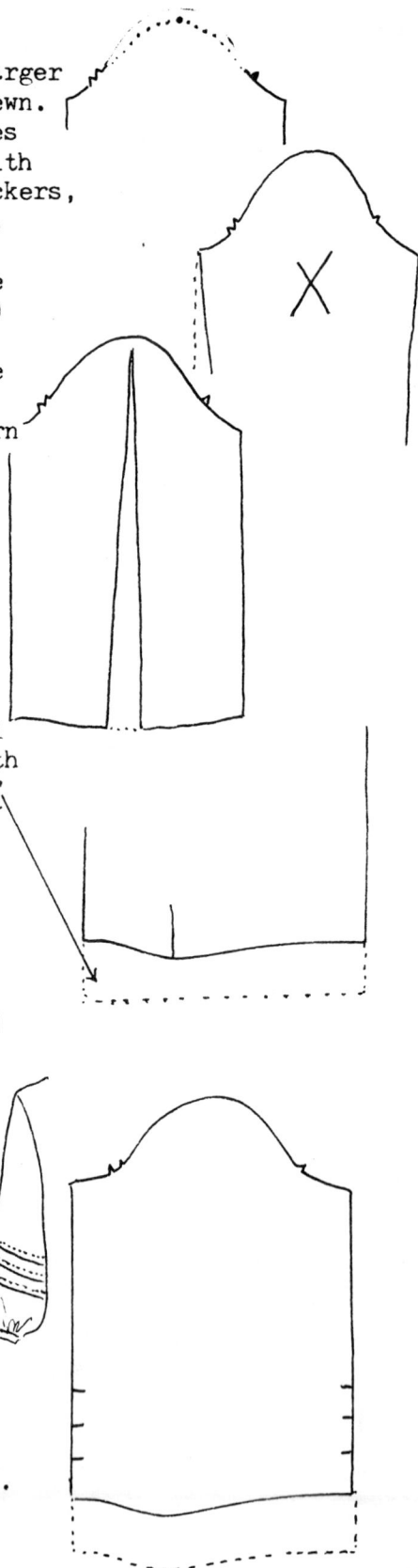

Roll-up sleeves. Sleeves on the basic
blouse can, of course, be rolled up for
a convertible treatment. But if the sleeves
will always be rolled up, there is no need
of the extra work and time put into making
the cuff and attaching it. Cut a straight
lower edge wherever desired. The hemming
of it has two choices:

1. A tiny rolled hem stitched by
hand or machine before folding up as many
times as you like.

2. If the fabric is a print and the
wrong side is unattractive, a large hem
(maybe 4" or 5" deep) may be more feasible
before folding up into place.

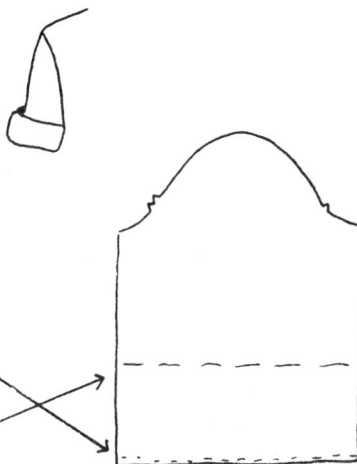

Short sleeves. Decide in a mirror where
the desired length will be above the elbow.
Cut the sleeve in a straight lower edge 1 1/2"
longer than this for the hem.

Keep in mind that this standard blouse
sleeve is rather generous in width. If too
wide to wear as a short sleeve, first narrow
by vertically making a fold in the interior
which tapers out to nothing at the cap. The
fact that the side seams would then not be
parallel demands that the hem flares to turn
up smoothly.

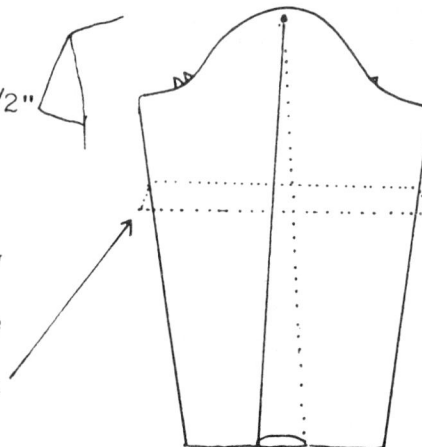

Button wrist, no cuff. Make this the same
as the example on page 31 for an elasticized
wrist. Be sure to cut off a straight bottom
for easy hemming.

When finishing the fabric sleeve:
1. Hem up in place (press under 1/4"
then 3/4" and hand or machine hem).
2. Sew a button 1/2" from bottom
in center of sleeve.
3. Try on and according to wrist
size, decide where to make two outer folds
and stitch buttonholes 1/2" from bottom.
4. Buttoning both buttonholes over
buttons will make a tight wrist.
5. Buttoning only one buttonhole
will allow pushing up sleeve to under elbow.

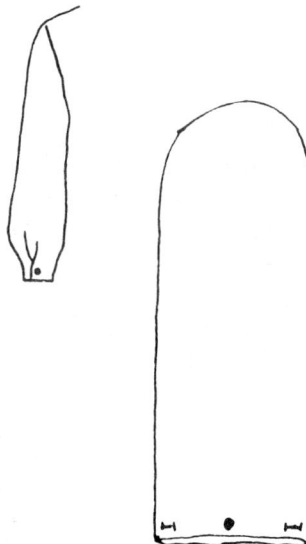

Full gathers at wristband or cuff.

    If thin, filmy fabric is used,
extra width may be desirable. To keep
caps smooth, extravagantly gathered at
wrist, slash sleeve from wrist to cap
at center and at front and back notches.

    Fan out wrist as wide as desired
and add the extra length dotted line
indicates.

    This can also be left loose and
hemmed rather than to stitching to
cuff for a bell sleeve.

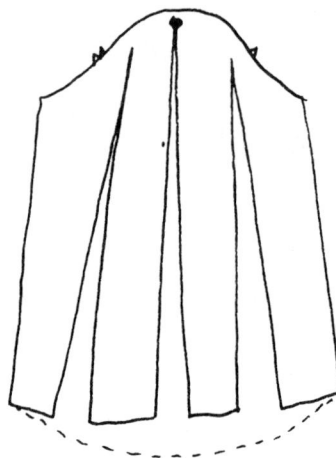

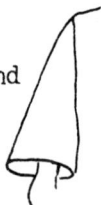

Pleats at wristband. Just make the
standard sleeve but pleat instead of
gathering into the cuff.

Narrow wrist, no cuff. Make vertical
folds at wrist tapering to nothing
at cap in three places: front and
back notches and center. Make this
large enough to slip hand through
when completed, or at seam leave
an opening for buttons and buttonholes.

    Lengthen 2" if hem, rather than cuff,
is desired being sure to flare below hemline
so it will fold up and hem smoothly.

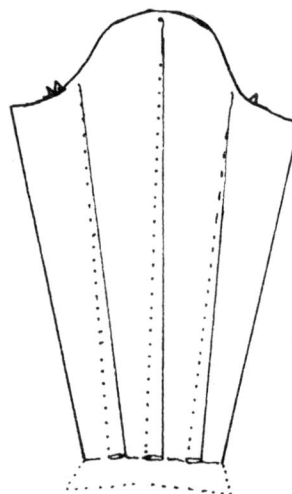

Seamed leg-o'-mutton.

    The above sleeve may be slashed
down the center with shaping added,
as well as seam allowances, before
stitching together.

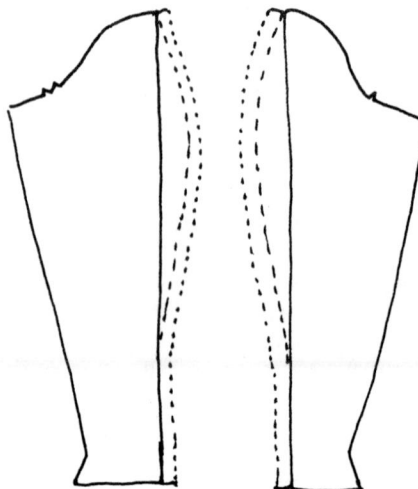

Puffed variation. Slash this sleeve
cap and spread wider, add length at
the top.

Sleeve back.
Sleeve front pattern
would be handled in
like manner.

After vertically
seaming it, gather in
excess cap fullness to
stitch into armscye.

If a narrower shouldered
look is desired...when pinning
sleeve into armscye, preparing
to stitch, begin at notches
and taper narrower (1" or more)
at shoulder.

Petal or tulip sleeve. This is a two-
piece sleeve which overlaps at the
cap. For this use two paper pattern
duplicates. Decide up in cap area
where the overlap will begin, and
the underarm length out at the side
seams. Cut one pattern layer with
mostly sleeve back, the other mostly
sleeve front.

Each of these parts may have a
tiny rolled hem at lower edge, or be
cut double with a tiny seam at the
lower edge before turning sections
right side out. Stitch underarm
seam while out flat, fold bottom
layer up in place, overlap right
amount at cap and staystitch in
place. Then insert sleeve in
armscye in the usual way.

It is also possible to join
the two pattern pieces into one
by overlapping underarm on stitching
lines. Then proceed with above
suggestion for rolled hem, or double
layers seamed at bottom, before
overlapping at cap and inserting
in blouse.

Or slash and spread lower edge for flare.

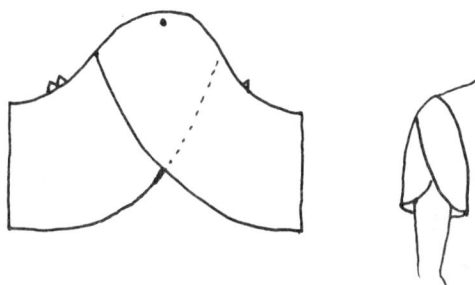

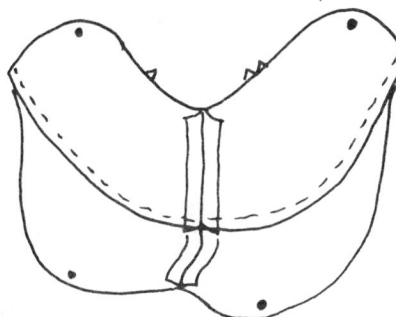

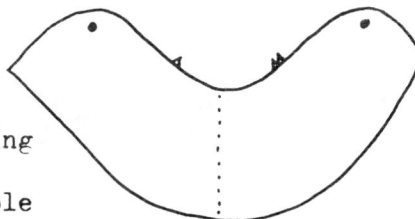

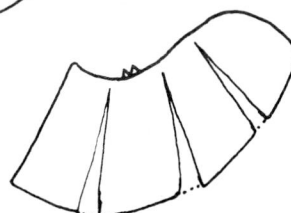

Puffed sleeve. Gathers at cap are achieved
by adding both extra width as well as extra
length so sleeve will actually puff round
rather than pulling flat.

Slash from cap down to wrist and fan
outwardly as far as desired depending on
the sheerness of the fabric used...more
fullness for thin fabrics.

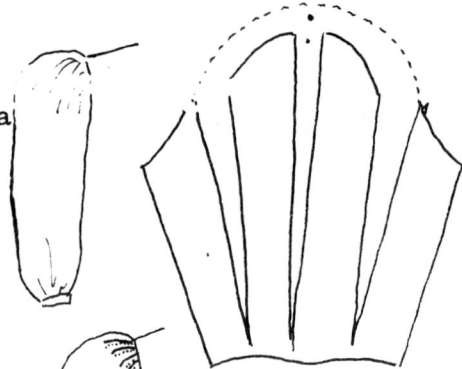

Tucked cap. Using the pattern just
completed, stitch a multitude of tucks
1" or more in length instead of
gathering the caps.

Full gathers both at cap and wrist.

.   Slash completely through the sleeve
length and spread apart. Remember to add
extra length anywhere fullness is great.

Lace or eyelet insets. Slash the
sleeve into two parts at the center,
or additional places if more lace
rows are wanted.

In fabric, finish likely-to-
fray edges before topstitching lace
in place. If no fraying will occur
stitch lace directly on top, cut away
away under fabric later.

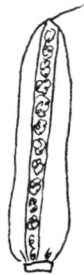

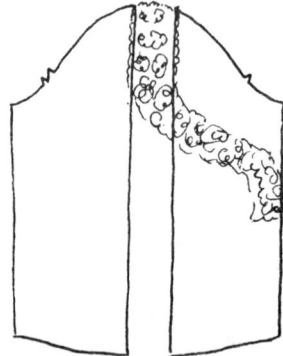

If you do not want skin to show
through eyelet or lace, merely topstitch
decorative row(s) (ribbons, braid,
contrasting fabrics are also possibilities)
to open sleeve before completing construction.

or refer to the
"move-it-over"
page 8.

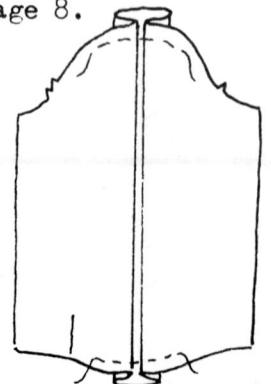

Vertical pleats. Slash down center
and spread apart. In the example
shown, if the pleat would be 1"
deep into each side, a total of
4" extra width would be needed.

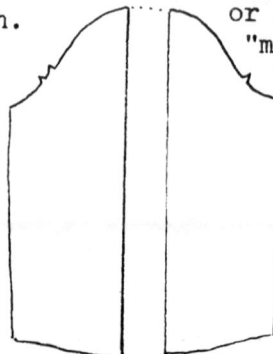

When fabric is cut out, press
in place and staystitch both ends before
completing sleeve.

Pleated cap. A little extra fabric
is needed to make pleats:
    1. One at shoulder seam or
    2. Two, one an inch or so on
either side of shoulder seam.

    This slight amount of extra fabric
is found by tapering from nothing at
notches to about 5/8" or so higher at
cap dot.

    When pinning sleeve into armscye,
pin straight underarm between notches.
Fold excess fabric into pleats in desired
locations when pinning caps. Uniformity is
better achieved if then the wrists are also
pleated rather than gathered unto cuff.

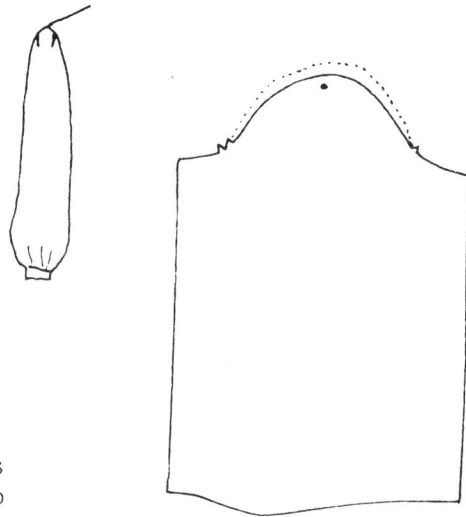

Deeply pleated cap. Add still more
heighth at cap to achieve almost a cupped
effect as the excess fabric is pleated
from outside, folded to center.

    This would be difficult or impossible
to later press so be sure the fabric used
is of a type that comes from the dryer
ready to wear.

    It may look more crisp if a duplicate
of this cap is cut from a sew-in Pellon
interfacing, staystitched under the sleeve
cap at seam edge, and pleated as one
with the blouse fabric to preserve shape.

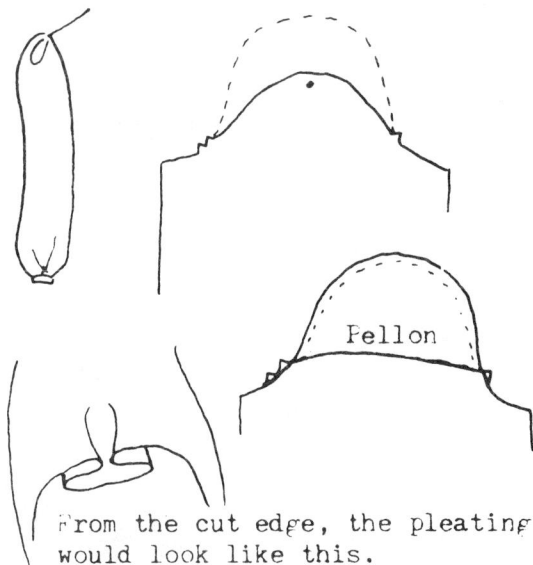

Pellon

From the cut edge, the pleating
would look like this.

Square armhole. Draw the square shape
on bodice front and back. It is also
possible to draw this line larger...
forther in toward neck on the shoulder,
and lower under the arm as illustrated
on the next page.

    Slash cut-off pieces from notches X
into corner to flatten out when taping
them to sleeve front and back.

    Add seam allowances both to bodice
areas and to sleeve squares on outer
cut edges.

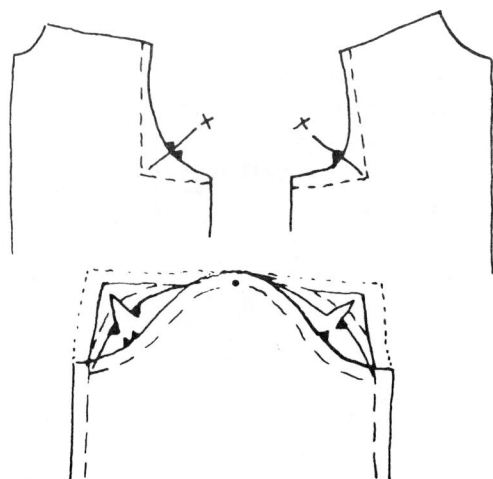

The first sketch shows square cut illustrated on p. 47. The second sketch is how it would look with a deeper cut. This shows up well on plain fabrics, often topstitched to accent the cut. Another way to show it off to its best advantage is through the use of contrasting stripes.

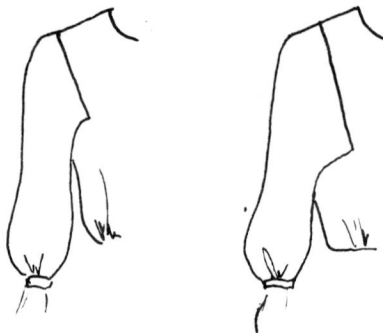

Pointed under armscye. The same method is used for a low point rather than a square.

When adding seam allowances on cut areas of sleeves, also smooth out sharp angles as small dotted lines indicate. This is to add a little more ease for lifting arm. The sleeve pattern looks peculiar, but it works.

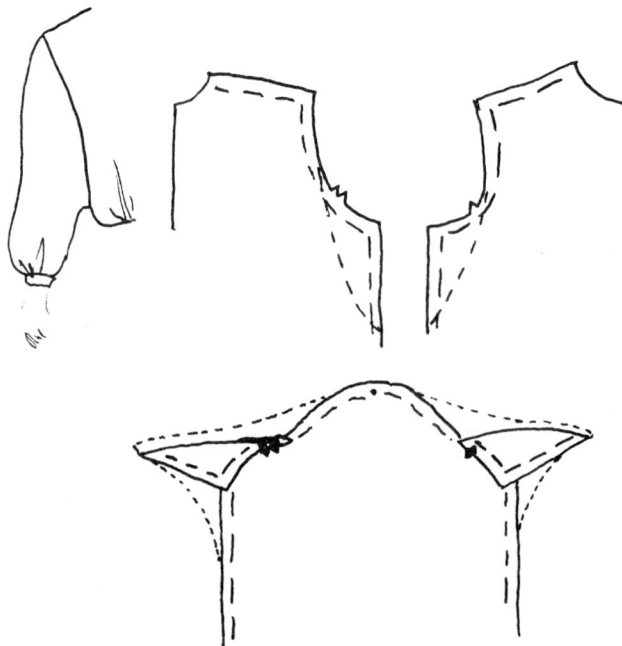

Dropped shoulders.

Whatever amount is added to bodice shoulders beyond the shoulder-arm point, is subtracted from the sleeve cap.

The notches are the transition points. The underarm seam is lowered and more width added for greater comfort in wearing.

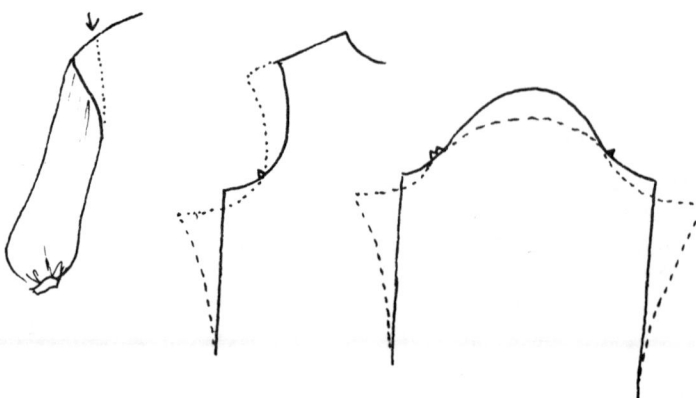

Another way to approach the dropped shoulder is to simply square off the shoulder seam and side seam, extending each to the point where they meet. Dozens of blouses can be created from this simple change without adding sleeves, since this automatically produces a cap sleeve for summer wear or a perfect shell under a suit jacket.

This would add about 4" in shoulder width so that on the body it would fall in this manner.

When constructing, stitch up this far and hem or bind or face arm opening.

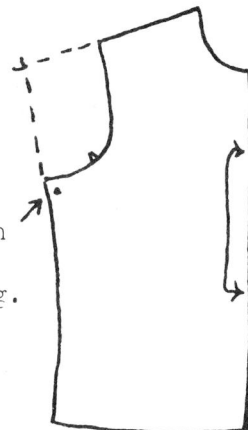

If a sleeve would be added to this, a corresponding height would be removed from the cap and about an inch of width might be added to the under-arm points at each side.

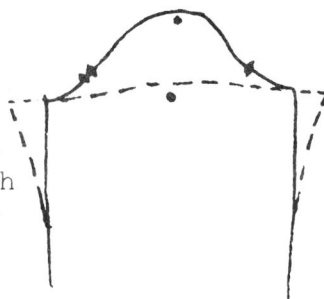

The sleeve is then usually inserted flat rather than in the round by seaming the shoulder and leaving the side seam open. Notice how the underarm points of bodice back and front drop somewhat with the widened sleeve. Do not ease in the sleeve cap as when dropped down the arm in this manner, it must appear perfectly smooth and flat rather than rounded or puffy. Stitch the underarm-side seam area last.

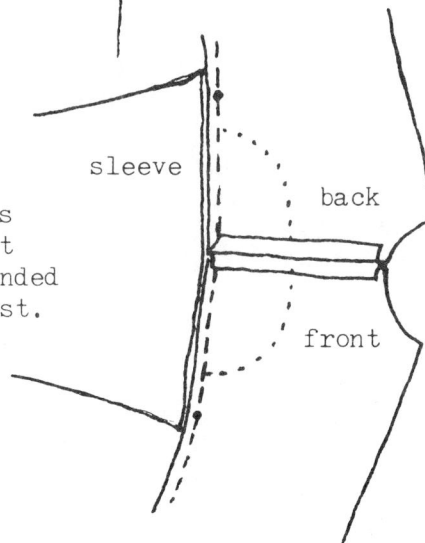

sleeve

back

front

The following are some other ideas for these cap sleeved blouses adding features found elsewhere in the book, or your original ideas.

Lace inset and sleeve edging.

Neckline cut out slightly lower, elasticized waist with tie ends, front opening.

Antique lace doily
cut in half with raw
edges enclosed in a
small tuck, accented
by twin needle
stitching, off-
center neckline.

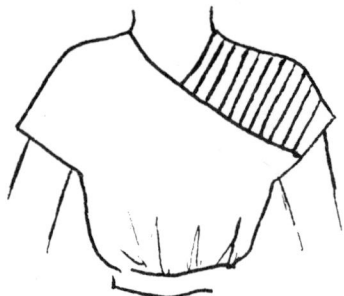

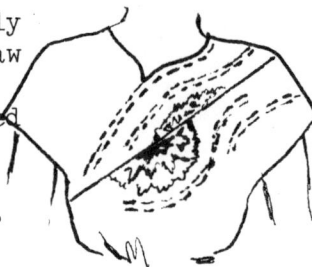

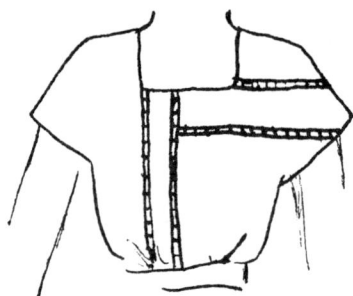

Pleated shoulder,
vee neck.

Color blocked pieces attached
together with faggotting.
Consult your machine manual
to see how to best accomplish
this on your particular
machine.

Overblouse with enlarged neckline,
one-shoulder buttons and loops. The
large collar has a scalloped edge
echoed at hems. This is done about
one inch from fabric edge with a
stabilizer underneath. Satin stitch the
scallops over pearl cotton, trim close
to stitched line after tearing away
the stabilizer.

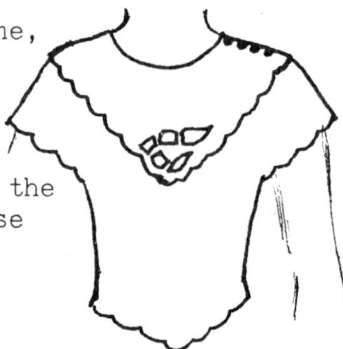

A vest or jacket is
made by lengthening
at lower edge, all
edges bound with
a contrasting
fabric or a
synthetic suede.

Bands are added to
sleeves cut either on
the straight or on the
bias. One side of the
surplice front is appli-
qued, quilted in place
with a little padding
between layers. Bind
neck edge with bias.

An attractive sleeve variation is an extension which
is stitched on the shoulder only to the shoulder point
dot, then all edges below that hemmed by hand or
machine. Tie the ends in a knot with a cool
opening on arm between shoulder point and
knot. The knot is tied before putting
the blouse on!

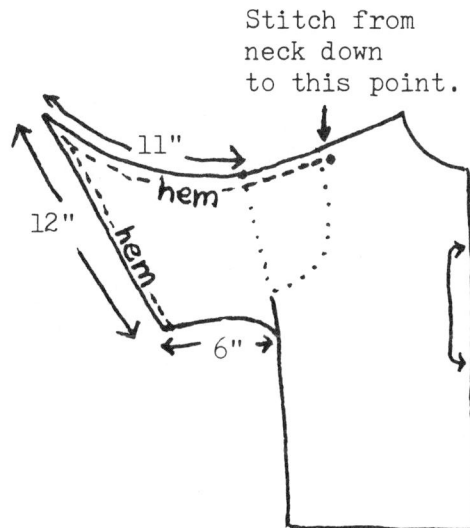

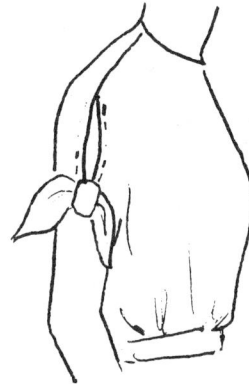

Stitch from
neck down
to this point.

11"

hem

12"

hem

6"

To make this idea into
a long sleeved blouse,
extend the sleeve all
the way down to a slim
wrist if desired. Lower
the underarm curve into
a batwing.

To decide how long this sleeve
should be made, simply measure
your body from the neck
point down to your
wrist and before
cutting decide
whether to hem, bind, or cuff.

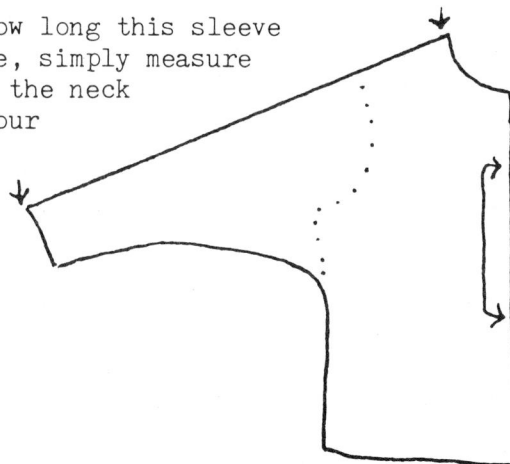

Now to get back to other
sleeve details...

Opening above wristband.

If sleeves will always be buttoned at wrist, never rolled up, here is a quick possibility. Where the cuff opening will be, clip 5/8" on either side of opening. Turn up middle section twice and hem in place before stitching sleeve seam and finishing cuff area.

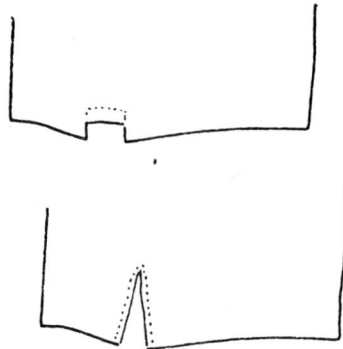

If sleeve might possibly be rolled up, a larger opening is necessary. This should be slashed 3" or 4", roll-hemmed under. Or apply a continuous lap strip before completing sleeve construction.

Varying depth of wristband. Your basic probably has cuffs from 1 1/4" to 2". These can be made deeper very easily.

When making changes here:
1. As cuffs become deeper, sleeves should correspondingly become shorter so the total length remains the same unless you want to leave the sleeve length as it was and have the sleeve blouse more.

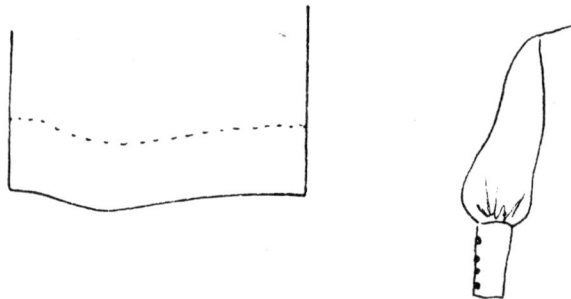

2. Extremely deep cuffs will need to be shaped as your arm becomes progressively larger moving up from your wrist. Slash and fan out cuff pattern. Cut two layers as a fold is then impossible.

French cuffs.

These are folded up so need to be cut twice the depth of original cuff.

They ordinarily utilize cuff links so buttonholes need to be made on both ends.

Here's an alternate pattern which only buttons through one layer rather than both. Either a button or cuff links can be used, but the cuff link would be hidden under the top layer.

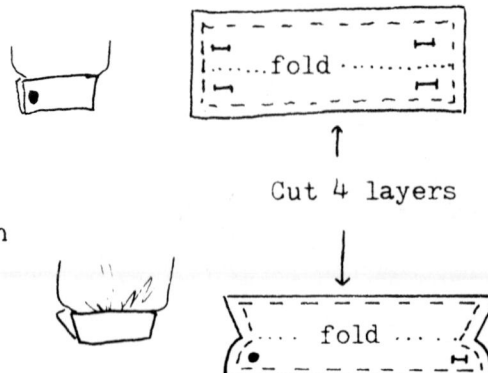

fold

Cut 4 layers

fold

Raglan sleeves, the second major
type of sleeve. The underarm
seam fits the same as the set-in
sleeve below armscye notches.
Above the notches some of the
bodice front and back shoulder
is removed and added to the
sleeve so the seam comes out
at the neck.

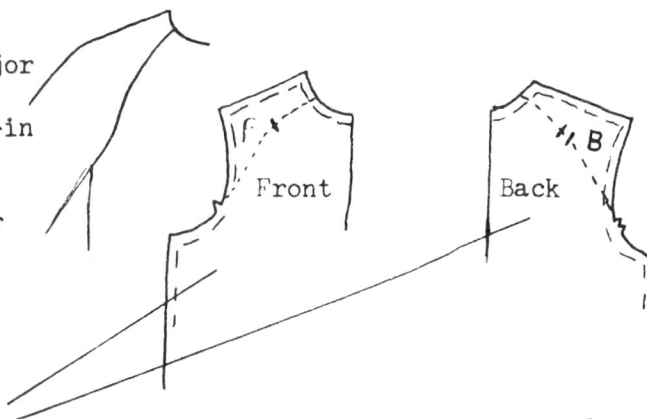

Front   Back

On bodice front and back
start at notches and draw a
flowing line to neck. Hash
mark before cutting apart and
identify so you know which is
which later.

Tape cut-off pieces to sleeve
being sure to match back with
back, front with front. At both
the notch and cap levels the
pieces just touch. Add seam
allowances to cut edges of both
sleeve and bodice back and front
and make notches out of hash marks.

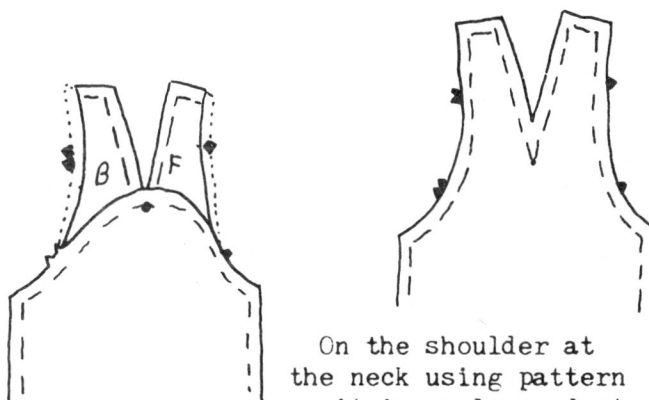

On the shoulder at
the neck using pattern
as it is, a large dart
can be stitched. The shape
of that dart may need to be
adjusted to fit your shoulder.

Another way to vary this
is to leave all the fabric at
the neck instead of cutting out
the dart.

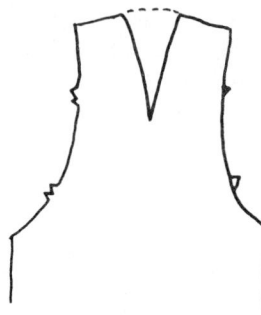

Then either gather
up that extra fabric
to fit the neckline....

Or tuck the excess fabric
toward the center like
a pleat.

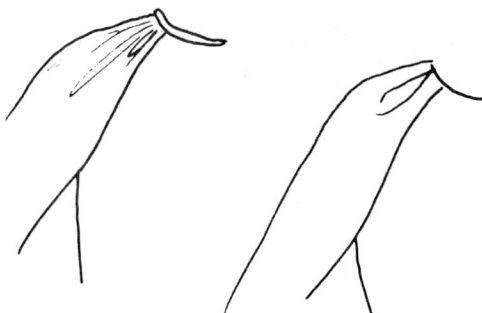

Shoulder pads.

If small pads will be used in these blouses, change the shoulder dart slightly.

Use as is at the neck edge, but taper shallower out near arm to allow space under fabric for pad as dotted line indicates.

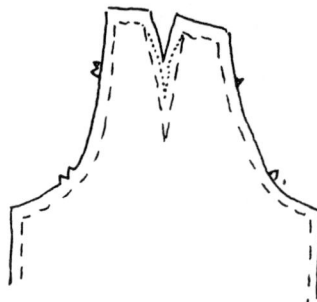

Raglan variations.

Instead of the curving lines formerly drawn in bodice for the standard raglan, more front and back will be needed to add to the sleeve.

Draw desired line and hashmark.

After cutting off front and back pieces, add seams to all cut edges and make notches out of hashmarks.

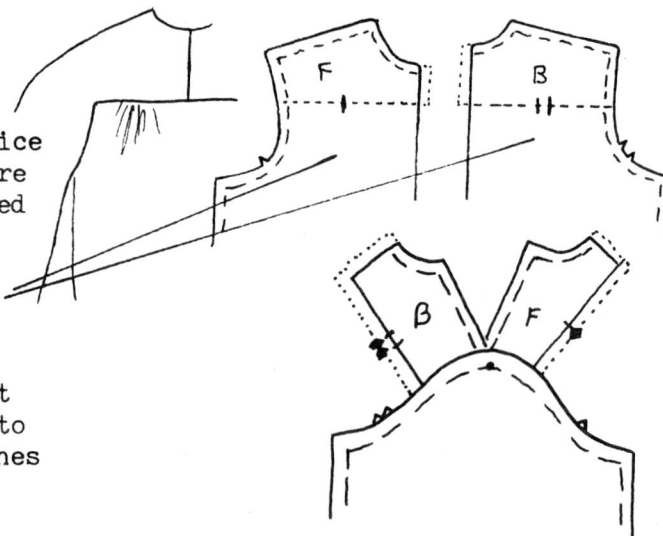

Then split bodice front and back pieces to add fullness ...fanning out to keep lower hem narrower, spreading entire length if more width is desired.

Don't forget to design a neck opening somewhere!

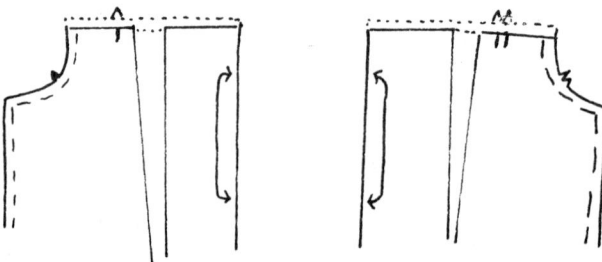

Square cornered raglan.

This is a repeat of the same process used before, just a slightly different design. I therefore won't use words....just examine the sketches.

Refer to technique section at back of book to see how to sew square corners in fabric.

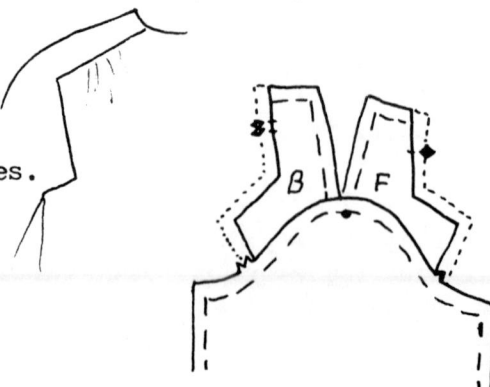

Peasant blouse.

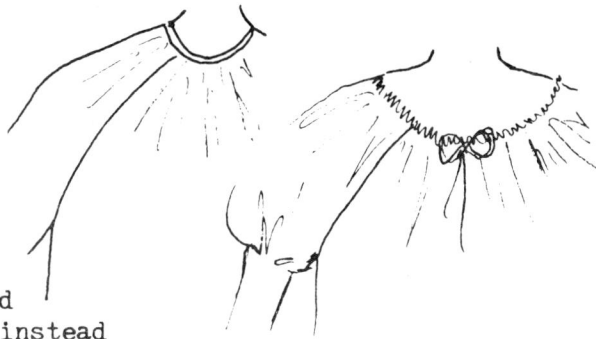

This is just the standard
original raglan with gathers instead
of the large shoulder dart.

To make the lowered neckline, cut off 2" or more from both sleeve
and bodices at the neck, slash pattern pieces to add whatever fullness
is desired. Fan out at sections where gathers will occur leaving lower
hem intact if no extra fullness is wanted there. The neckline can be
bound for permanent placement. A drawstring or elastic can be inserted
through casing to make neck depth or off-the-shoulder sleeves adjustable.

Kimono sleeves, the third major
category. The sleeve front and
blouse front is one pattern piece,
sleeve back and blouse back the
other piece. The only seams are
from neck down shoulder and sleeve
to wrist, and the underarm-side seam.
In other words, the whole front is one
piece, the whole back another.

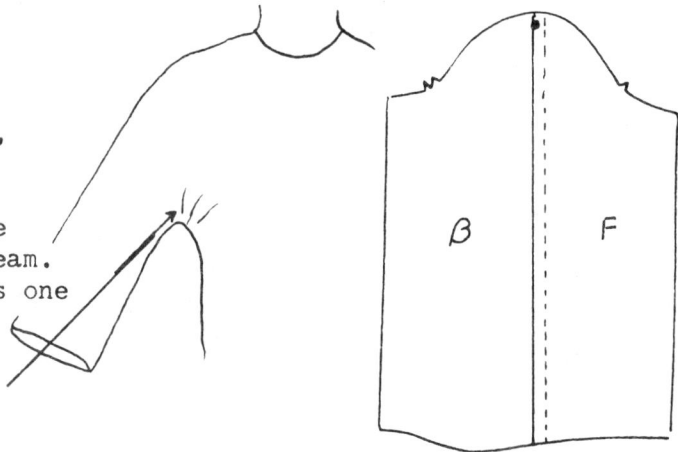

Underarm wrinkles in kimonos
are not only acceptable, they are
inevitable. These sleeves can be
changed in many ways you already know
...flared at wrist without a cuff, cut
off to shorter lengths, whatever you want.

First fold the sleeve in half lengthwise,
crease. Cut in two pieces parallel with this
crease, but 1/2" to the front of it.

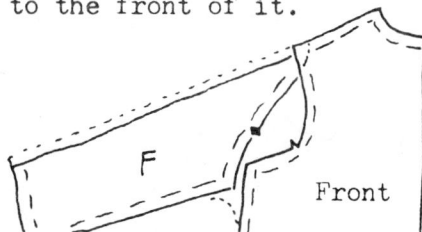

Using the sleeve front with
blouse front, sleeve back with blouse
back, overlap 1/2" at shoulder, lining
up sleeve and shoulder seam in a straight line.
Underarm, they will not quite touch.

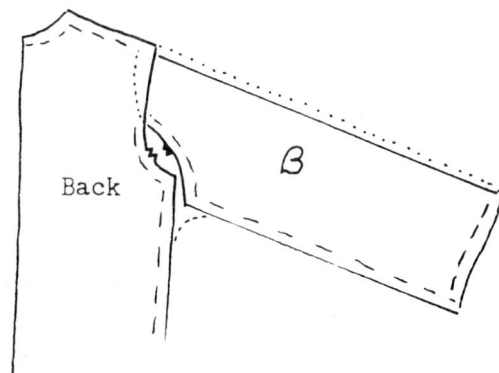

The underarm area may
then be squared off, rounded
out, or lowered into a batwing
sleeve.

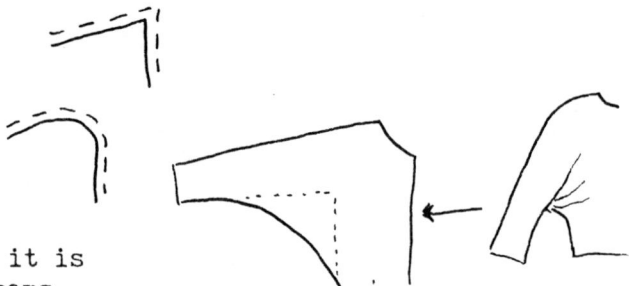

When cutting out the fabric it is
a good idea to cut 1" shoulder seams
from neck to wrist in order to adjust
back or front if necessary, so the seam's
placement looks right.

When stitching underarm seam, clipping will be necessary and possibly
taping (bias, hem tape, twill tape) for reinforcement.

Gussets.

These are little
bias cut pieces sometimes
inserted at underarm area
for greater comfort and ease
of movement if the kimono is
high cut in that area.

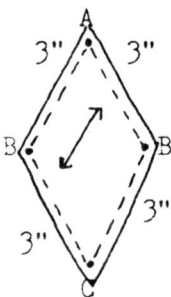

Not ordinarily used in most
fashion periods, at other times
they are a necessity to keep
underarm from ripping when raising
arms high.

The blouse seams will be
left open between dots A,B,C
so that gusset can be stitched in.

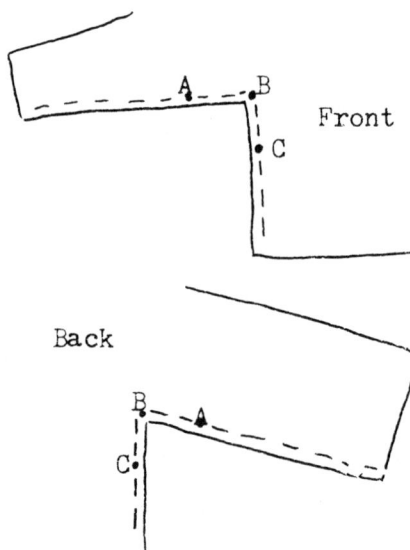

Straight cut shoulder-sleeve seam.

The kimono needn't stay sloped
between neck and wrist on the seam.
It's origin is in the orient where
they are generally cut out straight
from neck as illustrated.

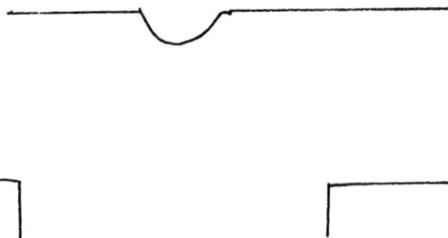

This entails extending shoulder
seam of blouse out straight from neck,
at right angles from CF and CB.

Line up sleeve part accordingly.
Lowering the sleeve underarm seam is
then necessary as these sleeves must
be very generous, not too fitted.

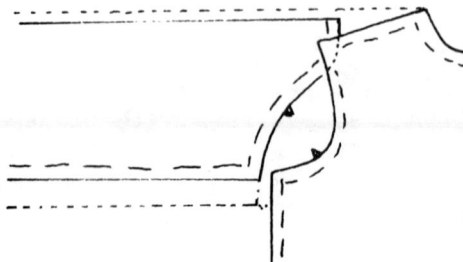

Front

Back

Banded kimono. To the previous process a band is added, maybe of a different fabric, to contrast color or fabric design. This band is made by measuring the total of back and front sleeve lower edges, making the band a continuous piece in a rectangle that length.

The band's depth is whatever you desire. Usually it is cut double depth so that the inside edge of band is hemmed enclosing their joining seam.

One-piece blouse.

This is possible if fabric is wide enough, sometimes made so by folding it crosswise and using the crosswise grainline rather than the lengthwise. It is seamless at back, front and outer sleeves (remember to design a neck opening somewhere). The only seams need be the underarm ones.

It can be made by the same straight cut shoulder-sleeve seam process already learned, just eliminating seam by overlapping back and front on stitching line.

This is necessarily a very loose fit and needs to be made of very soft or sheer, drapey fabric if used in a blouse with sleeves gathered at the wrists.

It can also be made of heavy or stiffer fabric if worn as a jacket-type top, or lengthened to a belted kimono.

Back

Front

One-piece blouse, alternate method.

This can also be done by arranging your original basic pattern pieces on the fabric as illustrated.

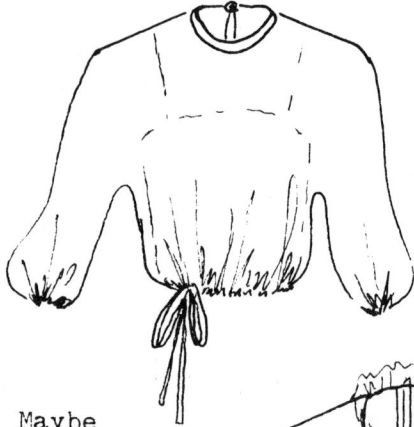

Maybe
sheer
overblouses

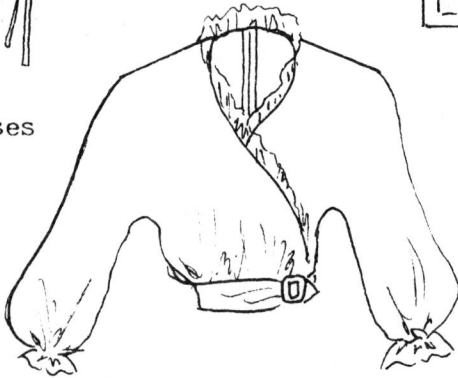

or traditional looking oriental kimono.

Either of the latter with their wrapped fronts would need to be cut with a center back seam.

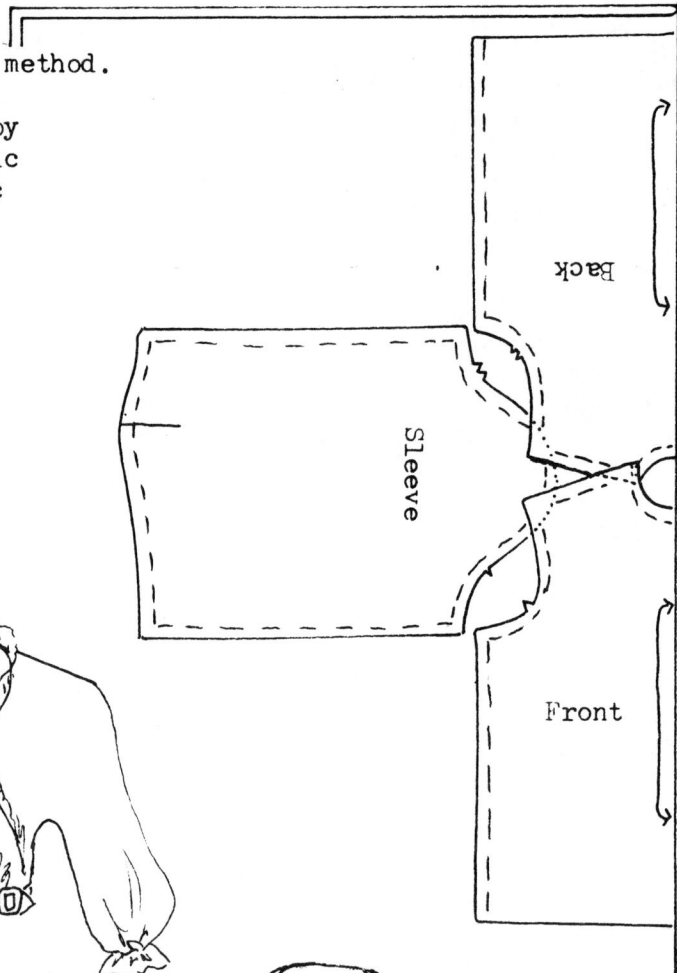

Patternless Blouses. Since we're getting progressively freer with the use of that pattern, let's go the ultimate! Many of today's simple yet beautiful blouses can be made without a pattern, working just from a set of measurements. These will have the minimum of seams and can be made in a matter of minutes depending on the treatments of neck, wrists, lower blouse edge...as in these fitted places is where the bulk of the work is located. Those measurements needed:

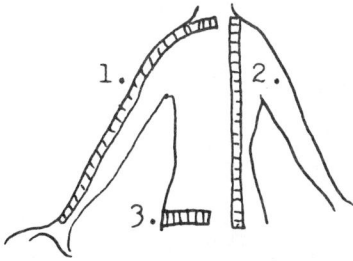

1. From the prominent bone (top of spine) at center back, over shoulder, and down to wrist.

2. From high point at shoulder down to waist or down to lower hem if a longer blouse will be tucked in.

3. Hip from center back to side.

To purchase fabric multiply measurement #1 times two. For example, if this measures 30", you need a 60" length of fabric.

To cut use fabric lengthwise, leaving it as folded from the bolt and place it on cutting table.

1. Pin to mark center of neck and measure out to wrist.

2. Measure desired length whether to waist or hip and mark this with a pin. If fabric is 45" wide or less, it will be necessary to cut it shorter hip length or piece it to increase size.

3. Adding some ease for gathers at waist or ease of fit at hip, mark width at lower edges. Remember this will later be pulled down over your head and must pass over your bust, so make sure the lower width is wide enough to slip over bust.

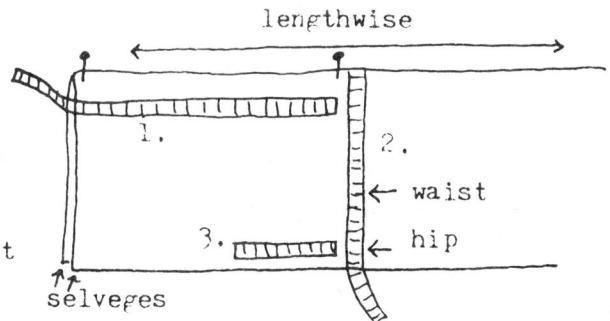

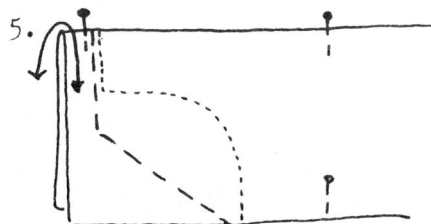

5. The lower sleeve hem must be large enough to put your hand through plus whatever extra fullness you desire.

Then cut on the------slotted line for a full batwing, on the........dotted line if less fabric is desired under arm.

Fold cut part over sideways at the center pins and repeat this cut for the second half.

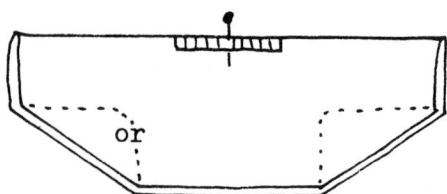

For the neck opening measure around
your head (as the opening must be large
enough to slip over) and cut a slit at
top fabric fold 1/2 this amount, centering
it on blouse. The basic blouse is now
cut out.

Some variations for finishing.

1. Sew up underarm seams, bind wrist and neck
with bias strips cut from those fabric scraps
or contrasting colored scraps.

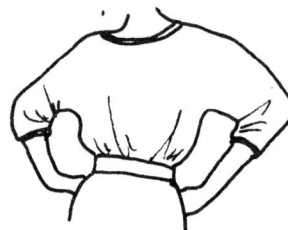

2. Cut wrist wider and 1" longer to begin
with, to accommodate pin tucks (maybe on a
striped fabric) and to turn up a wrist hem. This
is fitted at the wrist so the underarm seam is left
open a little at the wrist, buttons and buttonholes
applied. The pin tucks are repeated about 12-13"
across center front and center back at neck producing
the effect of puffed sleeves. Tucking of this sort is
done on flat fabric before underarm seams are sewn.
Because the tucking shortened the blouse
to waist length and nothing can tuck into
a skirt, bands were added at the waist front
to be buttoned in back, to the waist back to be
brought to front and tied in a knot.

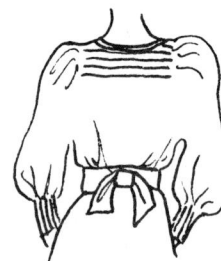

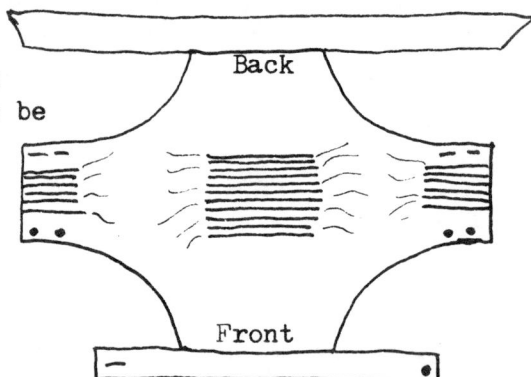

Back

Front

3. Cut several inches shorter at wrist to
accommodate contrasting color bands of whatever
width desired. Sew on the wrist band while flat,
then seam underarm and turn under wrist band hemming
to enclose raw edges.

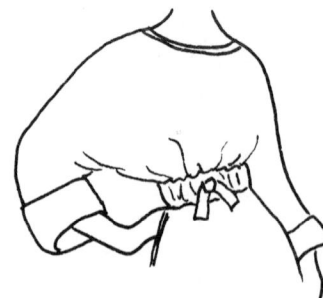

This was also cut off waist length but the
wide waist is bust measurement for slipping
over. Cut a waistband whose length is entire
circumference of lower blouse edge and about
4" or so wide.

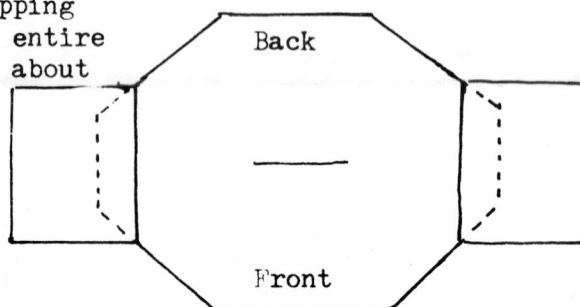

Back

Front

Pin and stitch to blouse with opening at center
front leaving a small opening through which a
drawstring tie will be inserted. Hem up
waistband enclosing raw waist seam edges.

opening

Cut the drawstring about 2" wide and a little
longer than waistband. Fold drawstring wrong side
out in half lengthwise. Seam edges and turn right
side out. Insert through front opening and draw up
when blouse is on to tie in a front knot.

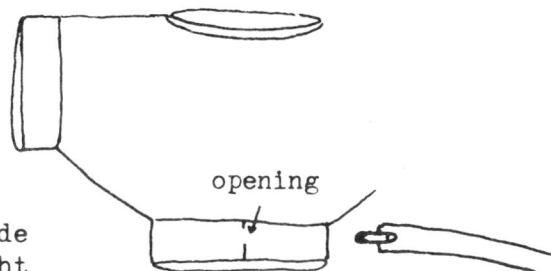

4. Color-block by adding pieces of other
colored fabrics or ribbons while blouse
is flat, before underarm seams are sewn.

Be sure all fabrics, ribbons are washed
to preshrink before beginning so no
puckered places will later result.

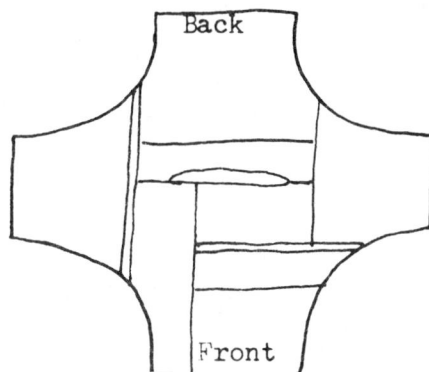

Back

Front

5. This has a high round neck made by
putting blouse pattern pieces on center
and tracing the front and back neckline.
Additionally, the dotted lines designate
the extra opening needed either back or
front to slip over head.

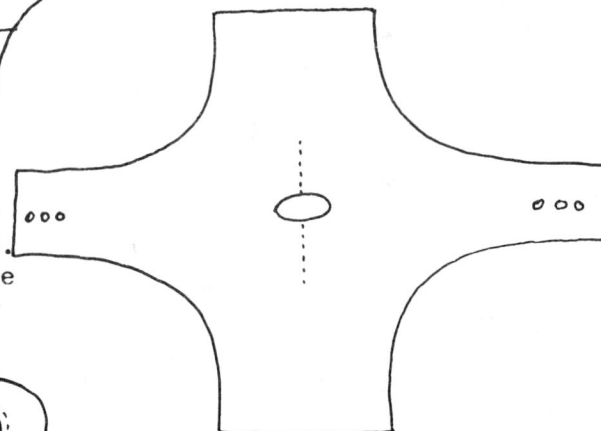

Then either bind this
opening or cut a duplicate
neck facing. Either way
loop buttonholes will
probably be used as
illustrated on pp. 71-72.

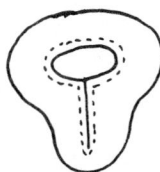

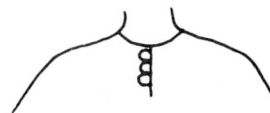

Wrists would have a
hem folded up, buttons
sewn at center, and the
loop buttonholes also
used here.

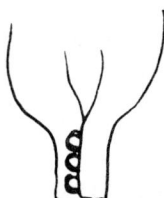

Such a plain blouse will depend on an outstanding fabric whose elegance can carry the starring role without embellishment.

If fabric length will not permit a tucked-in-skirt hip length, make a fitted waistband as illustrated on p. 29, but with the opening turned to the side seam.

It would also be possible to cut the lower hem with a front and back extension on one side, to be tied in a knot at side waist. For either the side buttoning, or side tying, a little of the side seam above would have to be left open (but edge finished) in order to slip down over bust.

6. An interesting variation at the neck would be using stripes or other contrast for a long exposed facing extending to the lower sleeve hem or band.

This strip would be 2" to 4" wide and complete wrist to wrist length. Pin <u>right</u> side of strip to <u>wrong</u> side of blouse at neck area. Stitch around the bateau neckline the proper size, trim out neck (clipping where necessary) turn to outside and press. Press under the 1/4" raw edges on both long sides of strip and topstitch in place.

Because of the generous cut and the drapey effect, soft, supple, thin fabrics work best for all variations of these patternless blouses. These are great gifts as exact dimensions are unnecessary and one size can fit a variety of women.

Look through fashion magazines and mail catalogs and discover how many of those blouses have been made in the same simple ways shown on these pages. These are also good places to gather many other ideas not suggested here. Requiring less fabric than more standard styles, these patternless blouses are a good way to cut down on yardage needed if the fabric is expensive. Quick to make and taking up little space they are also the answer to providing extra changes when packing for travel.

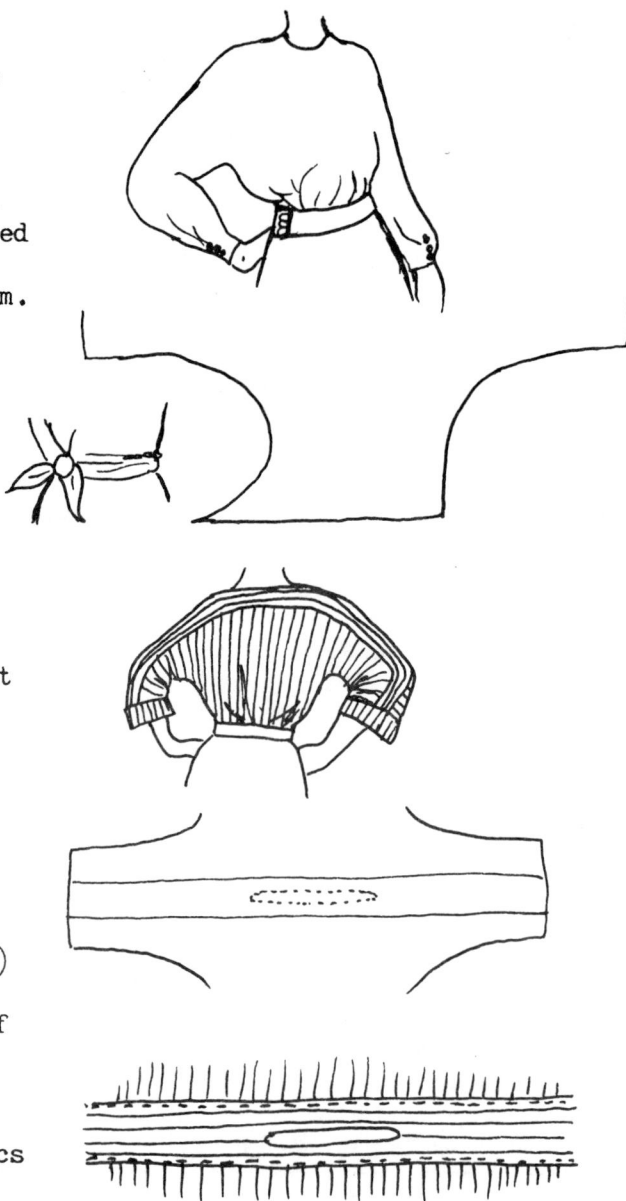

Fabric yardage too small for long
sleeves? These are elbow length with
a center pleat giving a fluttery
butterfly effect.

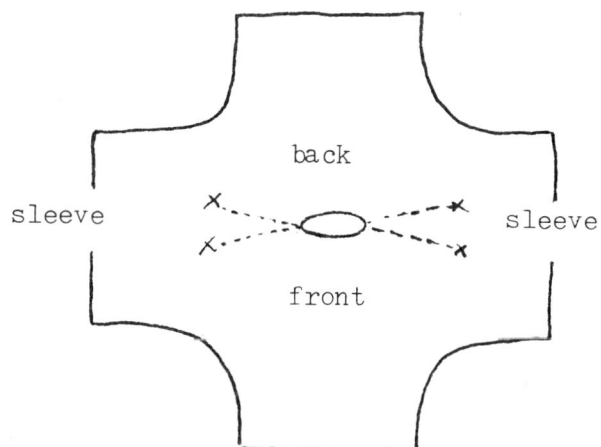

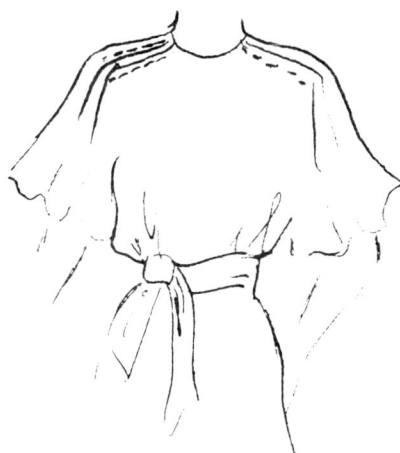

back

sleeve   sleeve

front

After cutting out, making
sleeve edges extra wide,
the original pattern was
placed on top of the fabric
to mark the shoulder line
slant both back and front.

These marked lines were then
folded to the center, pressed
in place so the back and front
folds met in the center, pinned
or basted, and top stitched from
neck out to shoulder point. The
sleeve hangs gracefully in an
unpressed pleat...perfect for
a summery feeling.

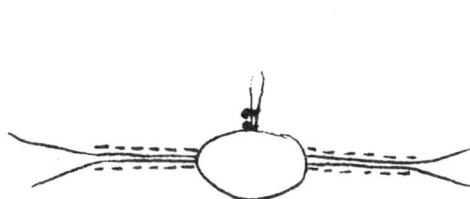

For winter do the same but lengthen the
sleeves and finish the wrist also with a
pleat formed by the overlapping of the
wrist buttons as previously shown.

An elaborately designed fabric is best left
intact, cutting it up for seams as little
as possible. This type then would be the
perfect candidate for a patternless blouse
to wear in the evening. The one sketched
on the next page is a see-through fabric
to be worn as an overblouse over camisole
and skirt or pants.

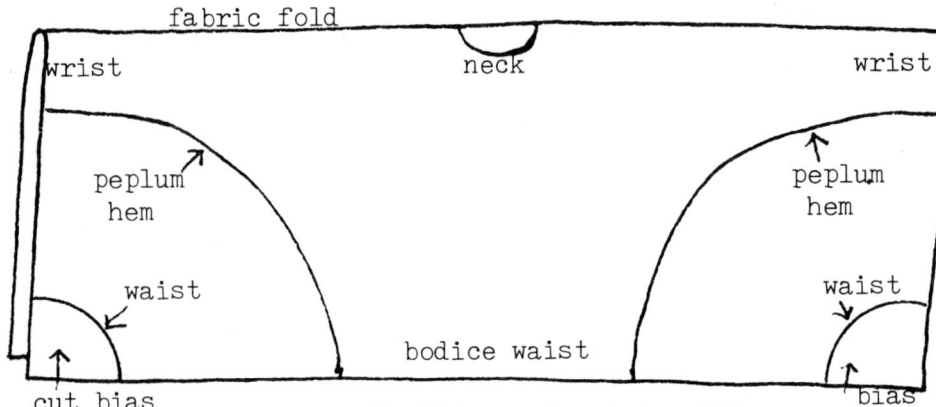

fabric fold

wrist   neck   wrist

peplum hem   peplum hem

waist   waist

bodice waist   bias

cut bias from these corners

Neckline and wrists will
be bias cut self fabric
binding and loop buttonholes.

After cutting fabric out as above diagram
indicates (not a scrap will be wasted!), the
peplum pieces are stitched together on their
straight edges. The resulting "doughnut" is
then stitched at the smaller inner circle to
the bodice waistline. Stitch a casing inside
the waistline to hold elastic and hand roll a
tiny hem at the lower edge of the peplum. A
heavyweight satin ribbon is used as a belt with
a flat bow and fringed ends.

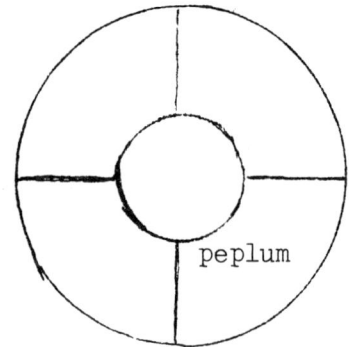

peplum

It is somewhat frustrating to
end this as imaginative creating
is my favorite pastime. By the
time this comes back from the
printer, I will have already
thought of at least a dozen
other ideas I wish I could have
included. But end it shall and
leave the rest to YOUR imagination,
YOUR creativity. By now you can see
anything is possible, so I hope you
will pick it up from here and have a
really good time with the challenge
of designing!

ADD-ON ACCESSORIES FOR BLOUSES

Most generally, and especially if you plan on it, there is a long enough scrap of fabric left after cutting out your blouse to make one of these accessories for extra versatility in wearing it.

With a long strip 30" to 60" and about 5" wide, fold in half lengthwise, right sides together and stitch raw edges leaving a small space in center for later turning right side out. Press, stitch opening closed.

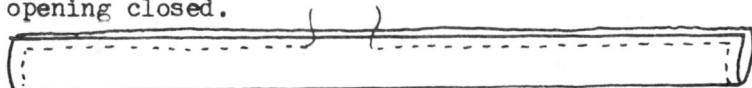

If it's long enough use it to tie a big floppy bow under a collar or double wrap a waist and tie in a knot for a belt or just twist ends under.

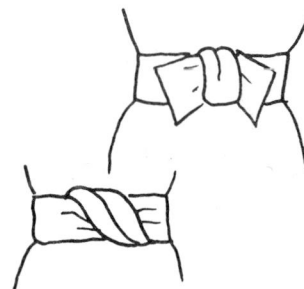

If it's shorter a petite bow will do, or a casual knot.

If it's wide enough tuck it inside the neckline for an ascot.

Or cut two layers of two different colors (compatible fabrics, please) and stitch all the way around ...again a small space for turning.

Loop that around your neck (fold at center through which both ends are inserted) and both colors show.

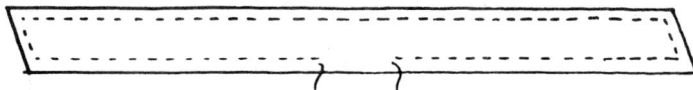

Or a small scrap to just go around a neck plus seams and overlap for button and buttonhole to wear with a wing tip collar.

Even a really tiny scrap can be stitched into a curved shape, buttonholes in either end. Sew little buttons in appropriate spots on blouse under collar to attach.

Add a cascading flounce (a sort of jabot) to that same curved piece to button under a rolled collar or over a mandarin collared blouse of the same color.

4"

9"

Cut two layers of fabric in semi-circular shape. On the three outer edges (leave small curve of neck edge open) stitch a 1/4" seam.

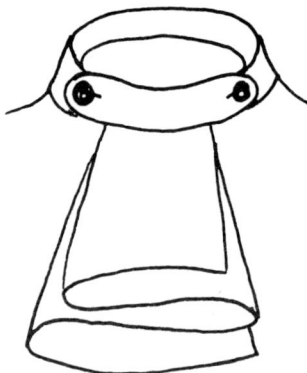

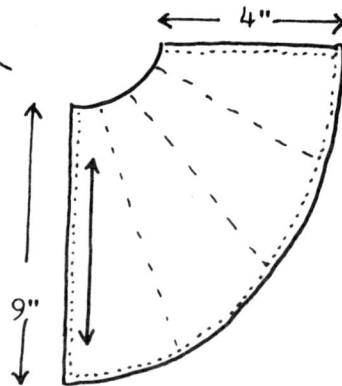

Turn right side out through neck opening, press. Accordian fold as dotted lines indicate. Baste upper neck layers together and stitch flounce between layers of curved neck shape.

This might even be made of organdy, chiffon, or any thin blouse fabric and lace edged. If the curved neck band is long enough to button to itself at the back of your neck, this can be worn with a suit and without a blouse. It might be wise to make the curved neckband wider in this case to better fill in the space in suit neckline.

Or that neckband, instead of being curved and fitted, could be cut on the bias and quite wide, gathered up in back where snaps or buttons would fasten it for a softly draped appearance. Thin, soft, supple fabric is necessary for this.

←— Neck measurement plus —→
overlap and seams

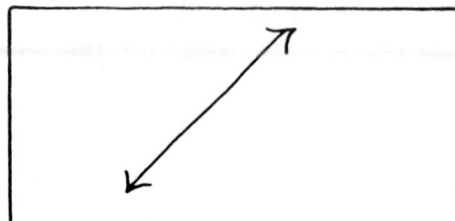

A cascade ruffle on a front band to button on in between layers of blouse right and left fronts is another possibility.

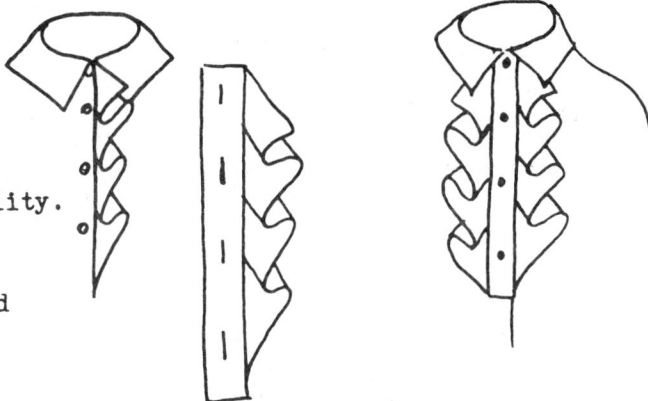

Or that cascade could be added to both sides of the band and buttoned on top of blouse rather than between layers.

Cut two layers and stitch outer curve, turn, press. Insert inner raw edge between two straight cut layers and finish its edges. Make machine buttonholes. Button between blouse layers if a one-sided ruffle, on top if two-sided.

Draw a complete circle whose inner curve diminishes to a point at one end.

The flat edge is the top, point on bottom. The measurement of the inner curve is equal to the length of the straight band. The band length should measure same as from the neck of your blouse down to somewhere just above your waist.

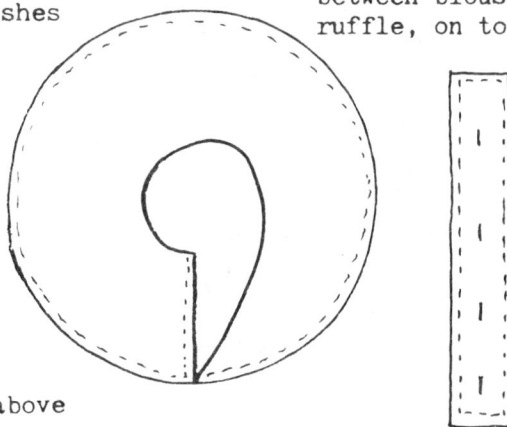

Use the same idea for a button-on collar on a collarless V necked or round necked blouse.

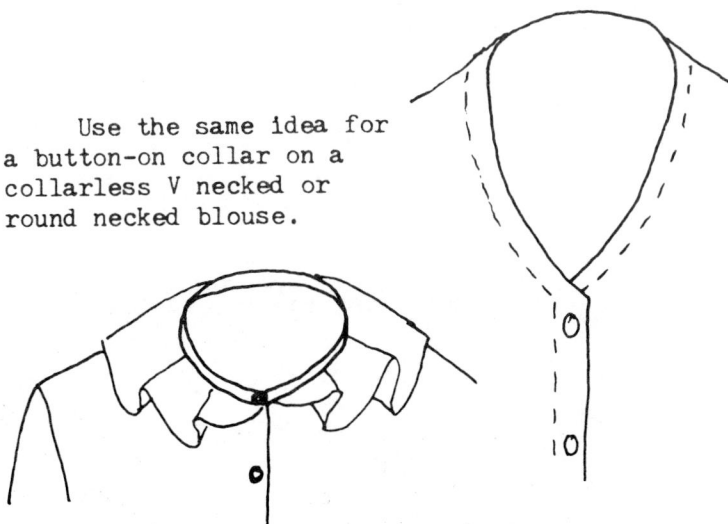

When you cut out your circular flounce make the inner circle measurement equal to your blouse neck measurement from center back to center front.

Cut four layers of fabric with this pattern.

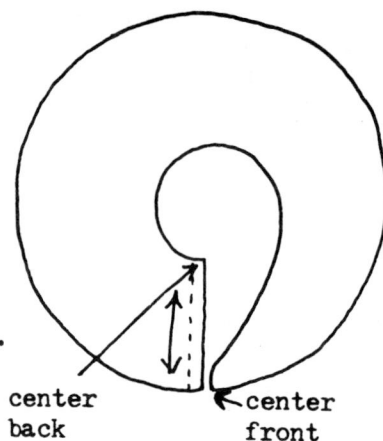

center back

center front

Seam two layers together at center back straight edge, right sides together. Repeat with the other two layers. Press seam open.

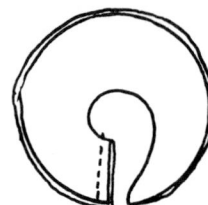

Right sides together, next seam outer curved edges of the upper and under collars (1/4" so no trimming is necessary). Leave inner circle (neck edge) open. Turn and press. Baste layers of neck edge together.

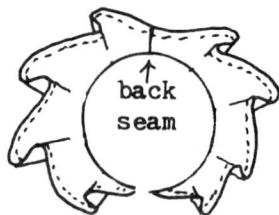

back seam

Cut a strip of bias 1 1/2" wide and as long as neckline measures plus end seam allowances.

Machine stitch one edge of bias to raw neck edge of collar. Tiny clips in curved neck edge may be necessary to get flat at stitching line.

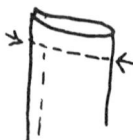

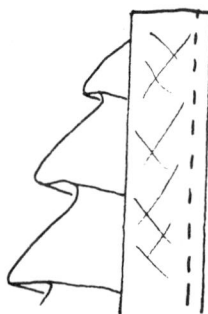

Fold ends of bias right sides together and stitch.

Turn bias ends right side out. Fold under long loose edge of bias and hand stitch in place.

Stitch machine button-holes in ends of bias. Button these on to top blouse button.

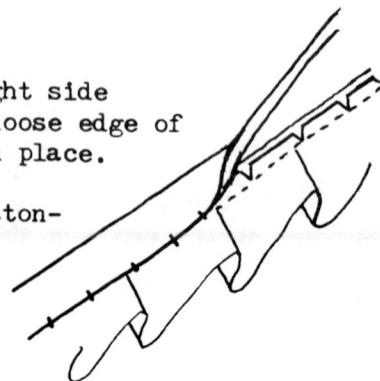

A gathered ruffle may
also be used as a collar on
a collarless blouse which has
a high neckline. If the fabric
is crisp the top part will stand up.

If of soft fabric, (such
as chiffon) both layers will
droop down.

It may even be interesting
...and especially if of a rather
transparent fabric like
organza or organdy... to
make double ruffled layers,
the outer one being slightly
narrower than inner layer so two
stand up, two down.

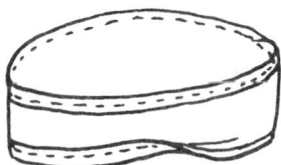

Cut strip(s) of fabric two to three times
your neck measurement (depending on how full you
want it) and as wide as you like. Seam the ends
together in a French seam so edges are enclosed.
It is now in a ring shape.

Stitch a machine rolled
hem around the outer edge.

Cut a piece of elastic a
comfortable measurement for
neck. This means not too
tight! Make sure when you
machine stitch ends together
it will slip over your head.
Stretch this out and pin at
intervals to inside surface
centered between edges.

Stretch this out
tautly and zigzag stitch
elastic in place. A free-
arm machine makes this
process easy.

To wear, just pull
over your head, elastic
side toward neck.

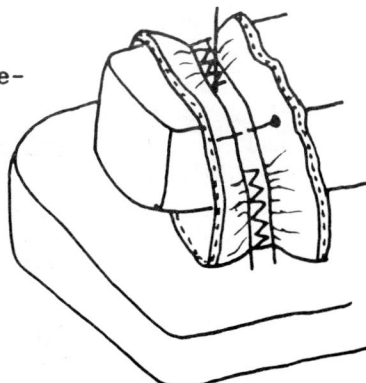

You might also use
this gathered ruffle in a
front buttonhole band instead
of the cascade shown previously.

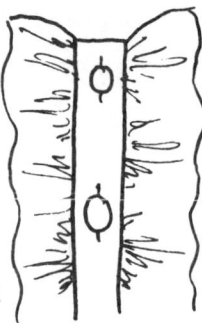

On some fabrics this
ruffle might be better to cut
on the bias instead of straight.
Cut twice as wide as the finished
width will be.

Fold outer edges to center and press flat.
This forms its own finished edges. Stitch two
parallel rows of large stitches down center.
These will be drawn up for gathering as well as
holding raw edges in place.

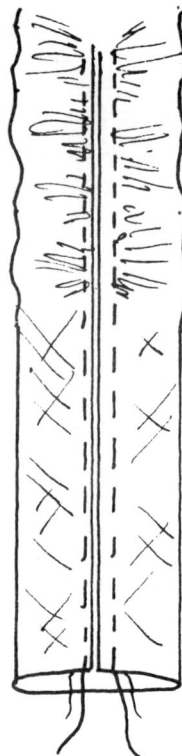

A funnel collar can
be made by measuring
circumference a couple
of inches lower than
high neckline it will be
worn over. If this measurement is large enough to slip
over your head, it can be joined
in a ring to simply slip over and
fall softly in place like a cowl neck.

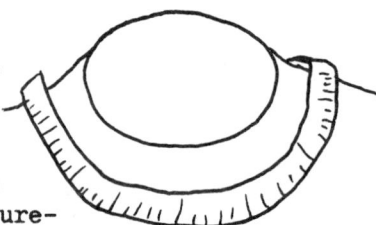

These are best cut
on the bias for a softer
look, so it drapes well.

Height is twice the
size desired when finished.

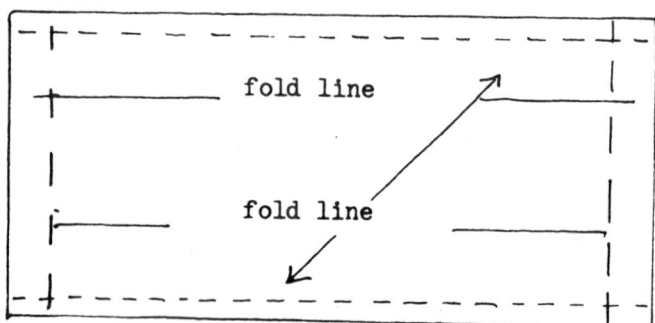

fold line

fold line

Fold in half to stitch, right sides together.
Press seam open over sleeve board or seam roll.
Turn right side out, then press flat centering
the seam.

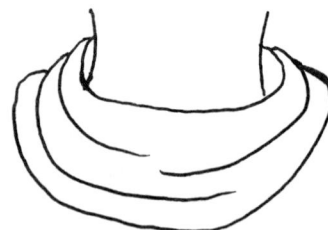

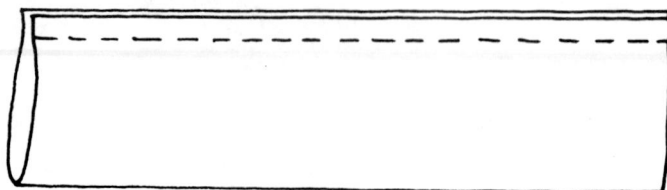

Bring open ends around
together and stitch two center
layers, holding outside layers
out of the way.

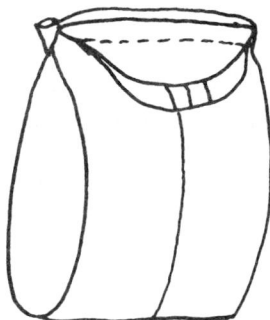

Fold the edges of two
remaining layers to inside
and hand stitch together.

Or that bias
collar might also be
done, not in a ring,
but finished out flat
with buttons and either
machine buttonholes
or fabric loop
buttonholes.

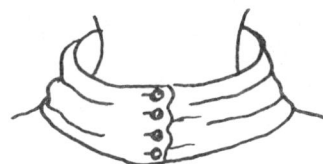

Wear buttoned up
or partially open.

Or if the scrap you have left over can
be cut in a triangle, simply make rolled hems
by hand or machine and tie a little
scarf.

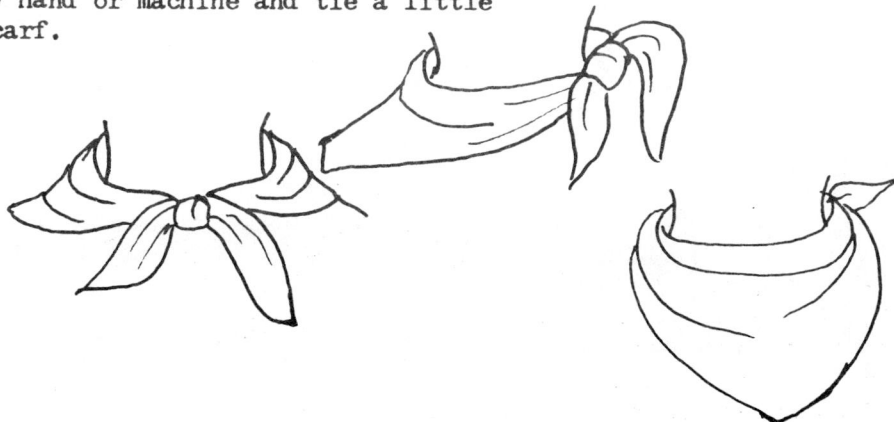

On a suit or dress a detachable
collar made of white linen or pique
is nice for frequent washing when
the garment doesn't need dry cleaning.

For example, from this
pattern for a shawl-collared
bodice front, cut four layers
of the white fabric where
dotted line indicates.

Right sides together,
stitch two layers together at center
back seam. Repeat with other two layers.
Press seams open and trim off shorter.
Right sides together, pin and stitch upper and
under collars together around outside style line,
(1/4" seams so they will be a little larger than
garment collar), leaving neck edge open. Turn
and press.

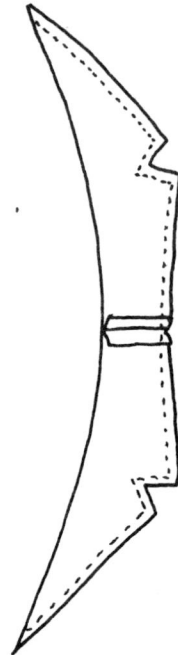

Cut a bias strip of the same fabric, 2"
wide and as long as the inner collar edge.
Use it to bind that edge the same way as was
done on the cascading ruffle on page 63.

Press bias binding under. Secure
to garment with snaps at center back
and one at each center front in
between layers of garment and
                    collar.

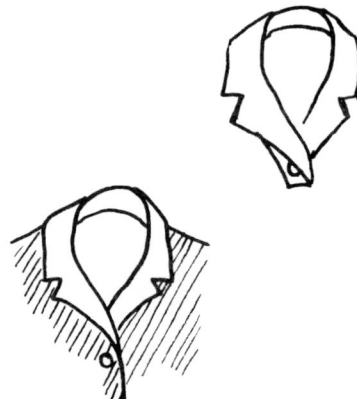

Dickeys.

These are actually the same as snap-
on collars except instead of a little collar
band, the bodice front and back pattern
pieces are used to make a larger inner
piece. Snaps are often unnecessary,
for it just sets in place on your
body under the blouse neckline.

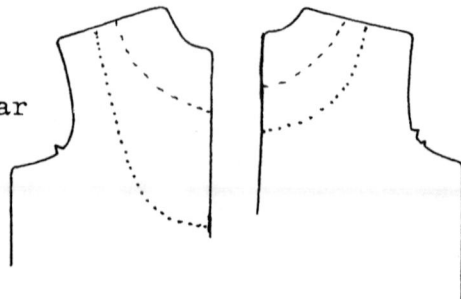

SPECIAL TECHNIQUES

Following are some sewing techniques which may prove helpful on
your blouse. These are included here to clarify processes mentioned
throughout the book.

Seam finishes. The way you finish a seam is dictated by the garment's
use...whether it will be taken off like a jacket and others will see
inside it, or if always left on so only you know what's there! They
also are necessitated by the fabric, whether or not it ravels, its weight,
its opacity or transparency. Serge for speed when possible.

No finish.

    Some fabrics, mainly knits, simply do not fray.
Press open the seams and forget them.

Pink or scallop.

    Pinking or scalloping shears may be used after
construction, not to cut out, for accurate construction
is more difficult on previously pinked edges. This works
fine if fabric ravels very little and will receive light
wear. Dozens of washings later, the tiny cut yarns may
be worn off and major fraying could begin if this
finish was not enough for the fabric.

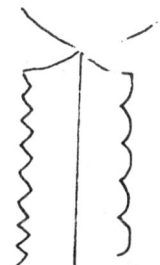

Turn and stitch.

    This is used if fabric is fairly firm and of
medium weight. Remember this involves treating
the seam three times: the initial joining before
pressing open, then hemming under each of the two
seam allowances. Appropriate for some fabrics,
for others a different finish may save time.

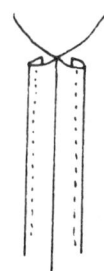

Bound.

    Two great commercial products are "Seam Saver"
and "Seams Great". These are both a thin knit tricot
about 5/8" in width, purchased rolled in a package.
The color choice is limited but they are so transparent
it barely shows. To use, do not press seams open.
Instead trim both layers down to about 1/4" and bind
the two together. It is a good idea to use a serpentine
stitch to insure catching the under layer.

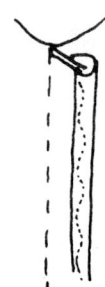

Trimmed and stitched.

Some seams do not press open and stay flat, but curl up. This is typical of some single knits. If so, stitch a second line about 1/4" away from seam. Trim close to stitching and press seams to one side.

Overedge

If the above conditions are true but additionally, the raw edge could fray or run, it is best to finish the edges together in whatever stitch pattern your machine is capable of doing. This is a good treatment if fabric is opaque. Transparent fabrics might look better more delicately handled.

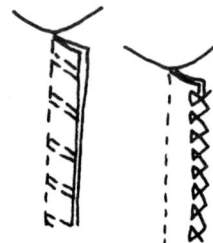

French.

This is a self enclosed seam and very good on sheer fabrics if the seam is straight rather than curved. It is a two-step method.
1. Put wrong sides of the fabric together and stitch a 3/8" seam. Press to one side and trim. ...less than 1/4". Turn and press a crease so the former stitching line is right out at the edge of the crease, and the short raw edges are enclosed. The right sides of the fabric are now together.
2. On machine, stitch a second seam, this time 1/4" from creased edge. Press to one side.

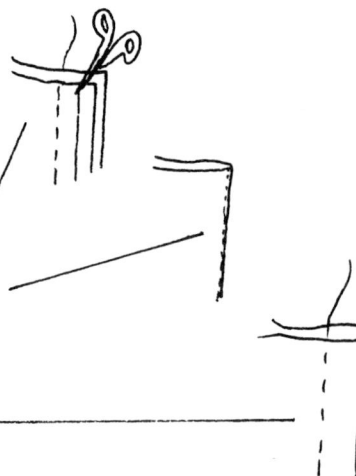

Inside-outside corner joining.

This is an impossible situation if incorrectly done. Properly executed it will look like this with a lovely square corner, but typically it turns out rounded and very amateurish!

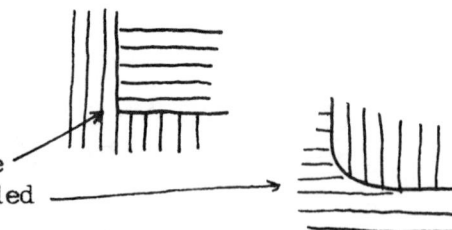

Here's how: on piece with inside corner there will be a large dot at the corner of the stitching line. With 20 stitches per inch, stitch through one layer not exactly on the stitching line, but slightly diagonally in the seam allowance up to the center of the dot. With needle down in fabric to accurately hold, lift presser foot and pivot. Replace presser foot and continue stitching diagonally through the other seam allowance. This is a reinforcement and needs small stitches for stability. The diagonal stitching in the seam allowance insures upon completion it will not show and will not need to be removed. Slash carefully exactly to, but not through, the corner stitching.

Hereafter, work with this inside slashed corner on top, the outside-cornered second piece underneath. First match up and pin the dorner dots exactly on top of each other, fabric right sides together. Then place pins holding the surrounding seam edges together. Stitch together making very small stitches (20 per inch) at corner area. At the corner, use the same needle down-to-pivot the fabric accurately that you used before.

Inside corner reinforcement
and slashing on single layer

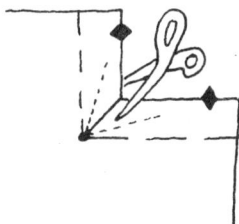

Slashed piece on top with
slash spread open so fabric
below it produces a fold of
excess.

Inside-outside Curve Joining.

This construction detail occurs in such places as joining the collar to the neckline of the blouse. The technique is similar to the corner joining. First reinforce the inside curve, the neckline edge, by stay-stitching the single layer 1/2" from the raw edge. Clip at intervals up to the stitching line. With this clipped layer on top, outside curve layer on the bottom, flare out so that clips open and edges of both layers are together while pinning and stitching. When pressing the seam open (if it will be opened...usually at a collar joining it is not, both seams being pressed into the collar) notch the outside curved edge only if necessary to keep fabric flat.

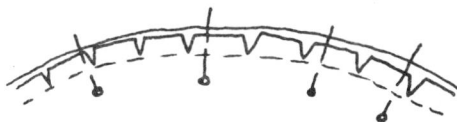

Edge-stitching Corners in Collars and Cuffs.

Here's a neat little trick to remove frustration when stitching quite close to edges. The problem is that when you approach the corner, straight stitching may be difficult to control without running off the edge. After turning that corner, it generally gets hung-up down in the feed dog where the needle pushes it.

Thread a hand needle so it is double, no knot tied, with 14" or so of thread. As you approach the corner, put hand needle through the fabric corner and pull out so you are holding tautly in front of you all 4 strands of thread and can guide and control into straight stitching.

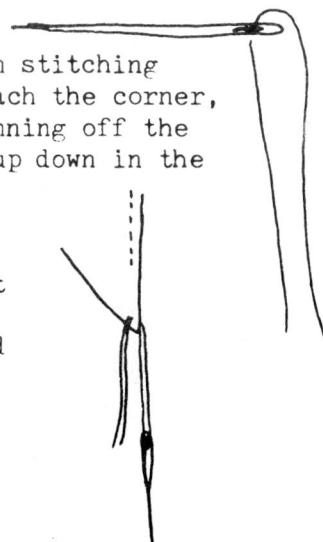

When you reach the corner, hold fabric in place with machine needle down as you raise the foot and pivot fabric. Then pull those thread strands tautly to back of machine while you lower the foot and resume stitching. Pull threaded needle out when past the problem area and have it ready to use on the next corner.

Ease, gather.

When you want no fullness, puckers, gathers to show at seam but are only trying to work in a little excess fabric, it is called easing. This is typical in the cap seam of a smooth sleeve which should always be slightly larger than the armscye it will be stitched into.

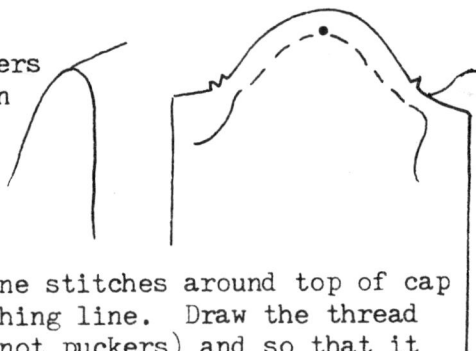

Run a line of large (6-8 per inch) machine stitches around top of cap from notch to notch exactly on the 5/8" stitching line. Draw the thread up only a slight amount so roundness occurs (not puckers) and so that it fits armscye while pinning in place.

Gathering is when you actually want the fullness to show and where considerable extra fabric is provided for that purpose. Run two lines of large stitching on a single layer of fabric 4/8" and 6/8" from the cut edge. Draw up threads until the gathered area fits the flat piece to which it is being stitched and pin in place at frequent intervals. Work with gathered piece on top to control fullness uniformly. The regular stitching line of the seam will fall between these two rows. Afterwards, pull out the gathering thread which shows.

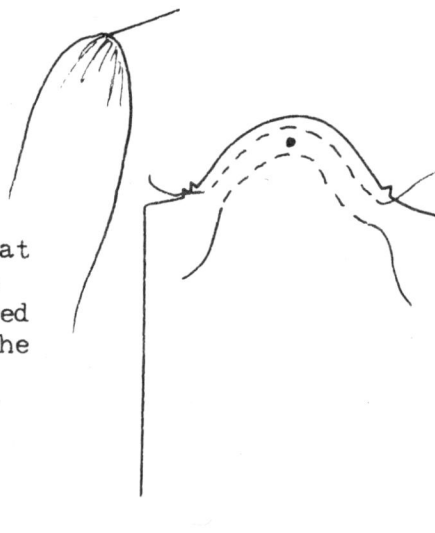

Fabric spaghetti or tubing, buttonhole loops.

Soft, supple blouse fabrics lend themselves to this process beautifully. In a woven fabric this starts by cutting bias strips. A knit fabric can have strips cut on the crosswise grain. The strips should be twice the finished width plus two 1/4" seam allowances.

The strip length is as long as is needed for the total number of loops times their individual lengths. If necessary, short strips may be joined with a diagonal seam as illustrated, not a straight seam which would be bulky. Press seam open.

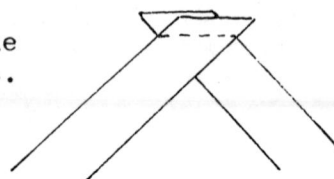

Fold strip in half lengthwise, right sides together
and use the machine foot as a gauge to stitch a 1/4" seam.
Remembering this will be a little stretchy, use small
stitches (15 or more per inch) as they have more "give"
and thread will be less likely to break.

Insert a loop turner (a marvelous and
indispensible little piece of equipment purchased
in notion departments) into wrong-side-out tube
with its little trap latch open. When hook is all
the way through to tubing's other end, catch hook in
fabric and carefully work latch closed so it covers
hook and will not further catch fabric.

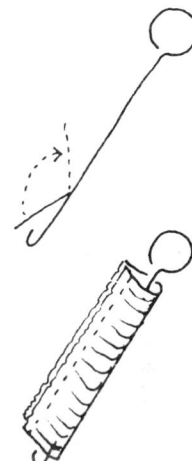

Slowly begin to pull loop turner while working
fabric right-side-out. Once you have it started, it
will turn quickly and easily. Cut this into the lengths
needed to provide room for button to go through as well
as ends (seam allowances) to stitch into seams.

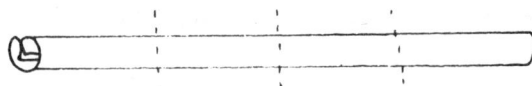

Buttonhole loops, after being cut are pinned
in place next to neck or sleeve opening in manner
sketched, raw ends toward outer edge, loops
toward interior. Cover this by facing, right
sides together, (this would mean the loops are
concealed between layers while stitching) and
stitch as indicated.

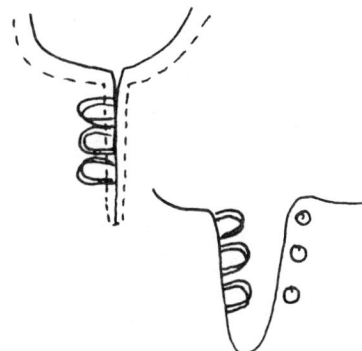

When turned right side out, the loops are
in the proper position for securing buttons.

Corded tubing.

If no stretch is wanted, cord these loops to stabilize. White cotton
or nylon cording in various thicknesses is carried in notions departments
for this purpose and purchased by the yard.

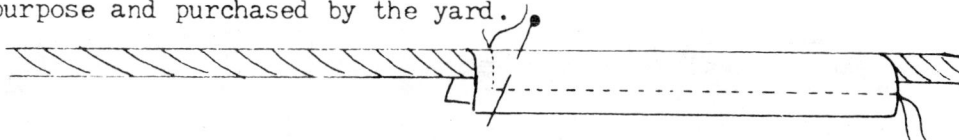

Cut bias strips same as for uncorded tubing. Begin with a cord
twice the length as needed. Fold fabric inside out over cord, leaving
uncovered cord length of fabric strip. Stitch across end to anchor, then
length of fabric using cording-zipper foot in order to stitch fairly close
to cord. Use tiny stitches so thread is less likely to break when being
turned.

Hold the cord end (as pictured above, hold right end). With other hand, begin to pull fabric down to the left side. A straight pin may be needed to begin the process, pinning point through fabric to pull, but avoiding pinning through cord. Once the turning is begun, forget the pin and just use fingers (and probably fingernails) to complete the process which turns easily and quickly.

The finished right-side-out tube covers the formerly exposed cording. The newly exposed cording is then cut off. With "fatter" cording and wider fabric strips, the same processes are used for belts or other purposes.

Inserting bias welting in seams.

This is a decorative addition to interior seams (such as bordering an inset yoke or bib) or exterior seams (such as a collar or down fronts). Packages of cotton welting can be purchased in a variety of colors and are found on the bias tape rack of a notions department. It is not a finished cording as previously illustrated, but rather has raw seam allowances projecting from it for the purpose of stitching it into a seam.

To make your own, cut bias strips as long as needed and wide enough to cover cording plus two 1/4" seam allowances. Fold strip over previously mentioned cotton or nylon cord, but this time...with right sides out.

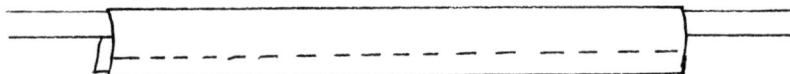

Using the cording-zipper foot, stitch close to cording with large stitches (6-8 per inch).

To one seam allowance on the right side of fabric, apply welting as illustrated by placing welting's previously machine basted line exactly on the fabric's 5/8" stitching line, raw edges out, finished cord toward the fabric's interior.

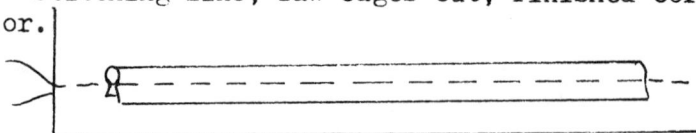

Use zipper-cording foot to machine baste in place exactly stitching over former welt basting line so it becomes as one piece.

Position second layer of fabric over this, right sides together, and pin seams perpendicularly.

Turn unit over so that former basting line is on top. Stitch the seam tracing over this line with regular size stitches. The welting will be perfectly attached in place in seam.

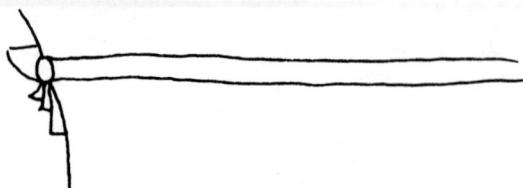

Shoulder Pads.

In some fashion periods shoulder pads are used in every type garment for a little extra "lift" and a slightly squared-off look. If planning to add these, refer to page 27 to see how fabric must be increased making room for them.

The filling can be layers of polyester fleece from any of the interfacing companies and here is an easy way to make them using scraps of your blouse fabric for the covering.

1. Cut two layers of fleece 5" x 3". Cut two other layers, slightly smaller.

(These pads would be just for dress or blouse, too small for suit or coat)

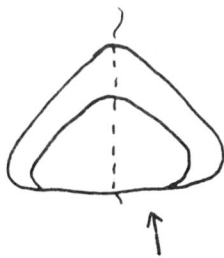

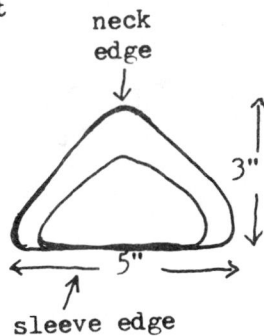

neck edge

3"

5"

sleeve edge

2. Using one layer of each size for each pad, line them up on top of each other and machine stitch together down the center (shoulder line).

3. On the wrong side of a scrap of the blouse fabric twice as large as the pad, pin shape, sleeve edge at center, and stitch all around to secure pad to fabric.

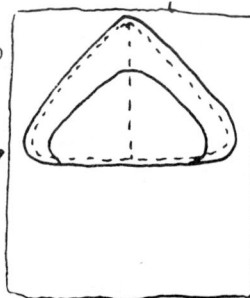

4. Fold in half, fabric right sides together, and stitch fabric layers only, around outside of pad, leaving an open space at neck point for later turning.

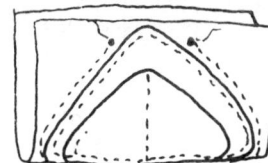

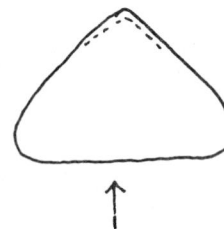

5. Trim off excess fabric, turn right side out, tuck to the inside raw edges at opening. Stitch opening closed.

or with a serger...

SERGER PADS

To cover purchased raw shoulder shapes with fabric by serging, cut a square of fabric on straight grain so that shaped pad fits on one half of it diagonally. Excess fabric is needed at edges for seams. Because that diagonal center is on the bias, the fabric will fold over and fit smoothly enclosing the pad between fabric layers. Pin in a few places to temporarily secure.

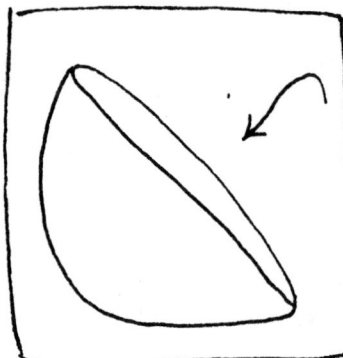

Machine baste flat edges through the two fabric thicknesses, slightly catching the pad edge. Remove pins.

Serge outer edge over machine basting and excess fabric will be cut away at the same time.

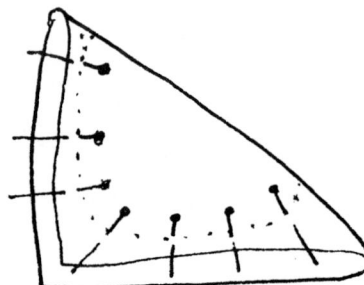

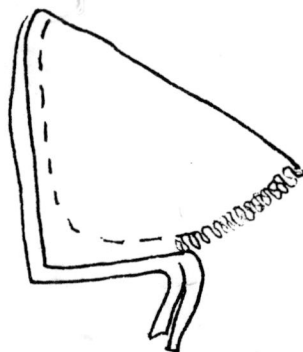

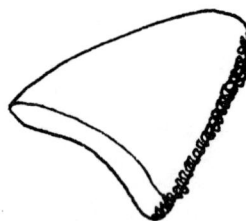